Anna:
Letters from
the Attic

Sally Anne Dare

Anna: Letters from the Attic

Sally Anne Dare

DeForest Press
Elk River, Minnesota

Published by:
DeForest Press
P.O. Box 154
Elk River, MN 55330 USA
www.DeForestPress.com
Toll-free: 877-441-9733

Richard DeForest Erickson, Publisher
Shane Groth, Editor in Chief
Cover by Michael Dear

ISBN 1-930374-03-8
Printed in the United States of America

07 06 05 04 03   5 4 3 2 1

        Library of Congress Cataloging-in-Publication Data

Fournier, Anna Delia, b. 1885.
  [Correspondence. Selections]
  Anna : letters from the attic / [edited by] Sally Anne Dare.— Rev.
and expanded ed.
     p. cm.
  ISBN 1-930374-03-8
  1. Fournier, Anna Delia, b. 1885—Correspondence. 2. Dare, Laurence
Albee—Correspondence. 3. Elk River (Minn.)—Biography. 4.
Minnesota—Social life and customs—20th century. I. Dare, Sally Anne.
II. Title.
  CT275.F6866A4 2003
  977.6'66—dc21
                    2003009541

This book is a gift for my husband,
Charles Fournier Dare,
and also to his siblings
Alan Dale Dare (1915-2002)
Donna Mary Dare Wiethoff
Mary Dare
and their families
in memory of
Laurence and Anna.

Further, I dedicate this volume
to two good friends,
Richard DeForest Erickson
and Shane Groth
for their gracious encouragement
and hard work.

Reflections

My wife's attic research has given me valuable insight into the personality and character of the mother I never knew, especially the depth of her spiritual life, the specifics of which for my own Christian faith I only came to understand in midlife. Anna's letters and Sally's extensive genealogical work have also greatly extended my knowledge of my ancestors and I learned that some people I went to school with were cousins.

Chuck Dare

About the Author

Sally Anne Dare lives in Elk River with her husband Charles and collegiate daughter Jenny Sue. She attended St. Cloud schools including St. Cloud State University, where she studied sociology, journalism and Spanish, and was editor of the College Chronicle in her sophomore year.

Ms. Dare was a reporter at the St. Cloud Daily Times, the Minnetonka Herald and the Sherburne County Star News, where she met Charles, her husband, the third-generation editor. On the death of his father Laurence Albee Dare, 90, following fifty years of publishing the family newspaper, Charles took the reins. In 1977 they purchased the Elk River Office Supply which Sally managed from 1977 to 1982. Charles retired then, and the couple sold both businesses to former Minnesota Governor Elmer L. Andersen.

Ms. Dare's interests include genealogy, family and related history. She writes poetry, reads widely, and is active at Central Lutheran Church in Elk River.

Sally and Charles continue to live in the Dare ancestral home, "Heartsease," at 1237 Main Street in Elk River, now identified as a Sherburne County Century Home.

Contents

Acknowledgments

This book, my first, represents more than just copying letters I discovered. Preparation for this project began, in truth, with people most of whom no longer live in this world, but who do live in my memory of them. I want to acknowledge some of them first.

There were certain teachers and librarians who from nursery school encouraged me to write. Some of my special friends were faculty families from the St. Cloud Teacher's College campus, now St. Cloud State University. The campus was quite small then, when I met many of these dear people. My dad was on the faculty.

My journalism and English teachers were wonderfully helpful in pointing me toward writing. I remember Mrs. West, St. Cloud Public Library librarian and also my first Sunday School teacher, as well as several children's librarians, both at the college and city libraries who offered praise for my poetry and always encouraged my interest in books. More than one quiet young person benefitted by their personal caring.

Later at Tech High School and at St. Cloud State College, I was deeply touched by one of many who "looked after me": Harriet Johnson, a Tech librarian who was also a mentor to me. After I married Charlie in 1968, we discovered that Harriet and her husband and daughter Susan, about my age, had previously lived in the house next door to my husband, Charlie's childhood home in Elk River. I don't know if she knew Anna, but she knew the Laurence Dare family well. So I wish to acknowledge Harriet Johnson as a profound force leading to this book, as surely as she represents all the special friends I had in St. Cloud.

There is a man who represents to me, and a lot of other people, all that is important and positive in Minnesota history. He has influenced me by his personal manner, in and out of business, by his active life and through our personal contacts at ECM at Princeton, and with regard to our selling of the Sherburne County Star News to him about fifteen years ago. Governor Elmer L. Andersen's lively interest in history on the local as well as the state level has demonstrated a high ideal to me with regard to the importance of history. Thank you, Elmer Andersen, for your dedication and high standards.

I wish to acknowledge the many folks of Elk River and Otsego who have offered information, history, and much help in the formation of my love of Elk River and Sherburne County history. Several who have been tremendously helpful include: Helen Gray, Stanley Wheaton, Bud Houlton, Helen Byson, Sally Thompson, Peg Reicken, LaVay and Hubert Wisness, Kirsten Anderson Clouse, Pearl Schenk, Alice Lindberg, Enoch Bjuge, Helen Houlton, Gladys Mansur, Bob and Hazel Hageseth, Wayne and Doris Trask.

A host of others, especially older members of the community who have shared with me their personal memories, photographs, and often fascinating stories of their earlier lives here may insert their names here.

Another special person in my life was St. Cloud historian Gertrude Gove, who was also my history teacher at Tech High School. More than any single teacher, Miss Gove gave me a lively interest in local history. She published much of her work on St. Cloud through the years and has been republished since her death. Her most interesting stories, to me, were about Jane Grey Swisshelm, the prominent Civil War years' publisher of the St. Cloud newspaper whose building was assaulted. Unusual as a woman in such a position then, Miss Swisshelm had all her type fonts and cases dumped into the Mississippi River by pro-slavery forces from out of town. I naturally imagined myself as a prominent editor writing powerful editorials and making a big name for myself!

I salute her as the kind of history teacher every young person should experience. Her lively interest in and presentations of history as storytelling filled my imagination, especially on the subjects of Minnesota and the St. Cloud area history.

My sincere thanks to Kurt Kragness of the Sherburne County Historical Society for his assistance in locating relevant information and giving practical advice on this new publication.

I cannot adequately acknowledge the individuals who actually made this work possible. As my publishers, Dick Erickson and Shane Groth, erudite and profound, yet humble and incredibly kind gentlemen, volunteered to edit and publish this book making it a successful venture for all concerned. I thank them and their families for their patience, interest, graciousness and generosity. I am proud to be published by DeForest Press of Elk River, Minnesota.

I wish to thank personally my pastors, and friends not previously mentioned, for all their encouragement and willingness to assist me. Particularly I wish to thank my friend of some 36 years, Betty Kickertz, with whose energy I can only wish I had been endowed, and who has walked with me along some of the historical and genealogical paths leading to this book.

I am highly indebted for his interest and assistance in the gathering of letters and for his terrific editorial help (we're both proofreaders, but he's the best), to my husband Charlie, who has been meeting his mother through the process of selection of certain letters I have shared with him.

Fournier Family (about 1896)
Left to right: Joseph, Hubert (PePere), Anna Delia (Fournier) Dare, Frankie
(died in 1897), Adele (DeMars) Fournier (MeMere), Benoit (Benny)

Publisher's Preface: Second Edition

We know that the sum total of individuals defines a nation, so the personal records that families are willing to share can be the best evidence of our historical roots. They become the statements of hopes, principles, convictions, disciplines that brought us to this point and which should not be lost.

Elmer L. Andersen

Elmer L. Andersen, former Minnesota Governor, statesman, author, newspaper owner, wrote these words included in a tribute to the first edition of Sally Anne Dare's book, **Anna: Letters From the Attic**. The title of Mr. Andersen's Opinion article in the Elk River Star News, August 1998, was "Sally Dare has made a notable contribution." We remember the pride with which Sally and her husband, Charlie, read those words. In his article, Mr. Andersen stated: "It has the makings of a fine epic movie or TV documentary with the Pilgrim and Acadian backgrounds, the political rivalries and pressures that caused people movement, and the bringing of people to the Minnesota territory. Then Anna's story of the seasonal struggle with the Mississippi and its log jams. There are several strands of mighty stories in the background of this tale of a gentle romance."

It has been our distinct privilege to publish this second edition of **Anna**, the expanded story, mostly told in letters. This edition includes the first book, which ended with Anna's marriage to Laurence Albee Dare, shortly after the bridge was built to span the Mississippi River. (For years Anna Delia Fournier had crossed the Father of Waters throughout the seasons, whether by ferry, boat, on ice, or on the congestion of logs.) This revised and expanded book celebrates the expressions of a French Canadian beauty who shares her world of imagination and industry. What she has left us in her words is a treasure that continues to glisten with the joys of expectation and discovery. Through her brief forty years of life, we are allowed to look into the world of a young woman at the end of the 19th Century and then to move with her into marriage and young motherhood in the early 20th Century. We also catch a glimpse of life during WWI and Anna's profound sense of the Almighty.

Anna's "letters from the attic" were actually found in the attic of the home of Charles and Sally Anne Dare, the historic family home in Elk River, Minnesota. Charles was the third generation owner and publisher of the Sherburne County Star News, a newspaper that was founded by his grandfather in 1882. The Star News is still in print after over 125 years.

We can be grateful that, all those years ago, a beautiful young woman wrote and received letters, that those letters were saved by a loving husband (a man of letters), and that Anna's daughter-in-law (one she would never meet) would find the attic treasure. Now, we are, again, grateful that Sally Anne Dare had the poetic presence to share Anna's letters from the attic...with us.

Richard DeForest Erickson
Shane M. Groth

II.

Tuesday.

Laurie— O, dear, I'm so anxious to have
you come again— Its so lonesome!!! I got
a new picture, to-day. Cecilia's. Awfully good.
Oh, I guess I'll answer your old letter.
    I meant that I had already told mama
———————hies about our trip and campi——

ELKRIVE
AUG
13
9 AM
1904
MIN

R.F.D.
SEP 8 P.M.
ELK RIVER,
MINN.

Mr. Laurice C. Law,
768 Cedar St,
St. Paul,
Minn.

Preface to the First Edition

Attics have always fascinated me. The first time I ever had one was in 1971 when Charlie and I moved into his family's old home in Elk River, on Main Street. There, abovestairs, I discovered a wonderful interest in genealogy and several other hobbies that still keep me ever searching for more details.

Among my discoveries were family trees, family letters, memorabilia from the 18th and 19th centuries, as well as all manner of diaries, keepsakes, and letters from as long ago as the 1850s. One is postmarked, "Orono," in 1877!

One box of letters has been especially curious and wonderful to discover. It contains over a hundred letters from a young woman to a young man written between 1903 and 1907. It was with eager hands that I unfolded these dusty accounts of the courtship of my husband Charlie's parents. Anna Fournier had written the letters to Laurence Dare who had kept them nearly fifty years after Anna's death, nineteen years into their marriage.

Anna's writings give us a rare opportunity to explore a first-person account of a period of major changes in Elk River, Otsego, Dayton and Rogers. In 1903 one crossed the Mississippi only by ferry, only in the right seasons and only on days when thousands of logs weren't pounding downstream, destroying boats or ferries altogether. There was frequent loss of life for the loggers. Until 1903 no cars had touched the dirt streets in this part of Minnesota, nor most others. Even telephones had never been connected to our community. Telegrams and trains sufficed for transportation and communication, buggies and wagons for more local travel. Passenger trains ran daily on a published schedule. Travel to Minneapolis and St. Paul by train was very common, as were nightly stopovers at city hotels and attendance at theatres, eating establishments, and large stores. It was not uncommon then for folks to rent livery rigs or use their own buggies and horses to tour exciting places such as Summit, Hennepin and Nicollet Avenues.

And it was in 1903 when two teenagers, students at Elk River High School, met and began the delightful correspondence which forms the beginning of this story. The lives of Anna Delia Fournier of Otsego and

Laurence Albee Dare of Elk River began to intertwine forever, in an old fashioned romance. Her letters to Laurence offer a touching and delightful account of a tender love story that grows between two very different communities.

In these letters, we meet members of the neighboring, largely French-Canadian community which included Dayton, parts of Otsego and other connected areas of Wright, Hennepin and Anoka counties.

Otsego, then a township, now a city directly across the Mississippi from Elk River, was already settled by Germans, Yankees, and others new to the area; but roughly between Dayton and the early settlement of Otsego "village," French Canadian immigrant families also had settled, since the late 1840s. Their spiritual center since the 1850s was in Dayton, in which St. John the Baptist Catholic Church stands today atop the picturesque Dayton Historic Village.

Anna Fournier was baptized, confirmed and married at the Dayton church, where French was the primary language of the members until shortly after the turn of the century.

Anna, who calls herself "a little French girl," was born at "Rogers Siding" in 1885 to her father, Hubert, born in New Brunswick, and mother, Adele, born in 1865 in Dayton. Yet Anna makes reference to "American people" who are among her friends. This demonstrates the unique perspective of many immigrants for whom it can take generations to think of themselves as citizens.

In fascinating detail, Anna's letters reveal much about those early years of a century we are now seeing to completion. Elk River High School, then on the block of the present Handke School, proved both melting pot and meeting ground for young people of the adjoining communities. Anna and LAD, as he was nicknamed for his initials, came from opposite sides of the Mississippi and unique cultures.

Otsego students then continued to rely on the old ferry to get to school in Elk River. For about fifty years or more a large squarish ferry connected the two communities. Anna's vivid descriptions of her crossings were typical of the dangers of the Mighty Mississippi from St. Cloud to Minneapolis, when bridges were scarce. Mr. Vassar was the ferryman; he had followed the Thomas family and earlier, the Nickersons, in that service to the community.

But in the years from about 1890 to about 1910 the river was often full of thousands of logs which were floated from more northern areas to the various mills along the river route to Minneapolis. Branded by the name of the logging company before they entered the river, logs were checked against that mark when removed for milling.

On the Otsego shore across from downtown Elk River, land was used by the Rum River Boom Company. It had other stations at Dayton and Anoka, and so on. Anna's father Hubert and grandfather Magloire DeMars had worked on the river. Hubert, a farmer, was called in when the fast-moving logs would begin to pile up. "Logjam" had a meaning less appreciated, but sometimes reenacted today in the form of logrolling contests. More than that ability, it was the job of the "Main Man," in this case Hubert, to locate that particular log which, if released, would restart the orderly run downstream.

In her letters Anna tells of weather-related dangers of the Mississippi crossing. Storms, freezing, and floods separated the populations. Anna complains of lonely, unconnected Sundays, and she gives some harrowing accounts of personal encounters with river ice. Every season brought with it unique barriers to education, transportation and commerce. She describes "anchor ice," thin ice, and ice forming as water froze around the little boat which, in winter, substituted for the usual flat ferry. Of course teams and buggies had few winter crossings except when the river was frozen hard. Low water exposed rocks.

What was really buzzing in the air on both sides of the big river was the need for a bridge.

Hubert and Adele, Anna's parents, moved to a large farm just opposite Elk River, across the Father of Waters, in about 1890. They farmed on the site of the present Lefebvre farm on Parrish Avenue, across County Road 39 from Christ Lutheran Church, and across Parrish Avenue from the Tom Thumb store. Part of the Fournier land bordered the Mississippi and the present Parrish Avenue.

Still, in those carless days, the area was quite undeveloped. The present Parrish Avenue was but a narrow path in some places, between the site of the ferry just east of the present bridge site. Otsego folks had to make their way through a much-wooded area full of wolves. Homes were not very close together, but the often interrelated families were, in spirit.

Anna's Ma, Adeline, or Adele DeMars, was the youngest child of the venerable Magloire DeMars, who had worked on and along the river in Minnesota since before 1850. He had once lived and worked in Itasca, a little place that time has passed by, across the river from Dayton today. Both Hubert Fournier's mother and Magloire's wife, Grandma Emelie (Cyr) DeMars, shared in common the Cyr ancestry, which Anna learns about both from her Pa and from her grandmother. Through this ancestry, Anna had descended from the earliest French (and English) settlers of Acadia, part of southern New Brunswick near Grand-Pre, French for Great Prairie, now called Grand Bay, in the Bay of Fundy just east of the Maine coast.

Henry Wadsworth Longfellow had memorialized that early community of French immigrants, people who were able to dam the ocean and farm the incredibly rich lands. In his story poem, Evangeline, Longfellow described a typical small village in which peaceful peasants shared not only French heritage and cousinships, but land, crops, fruit trees, and a common faith.

They succeeded in living on a land that others have not since been able to tame. They also lived in mutual respect and amity with the local Native Americans. This lasted from around 1620 into the mid 1700s when the British and the Americans took turns trying to claim their territory. During the French and Indian Wars, the land was finally claimed by the British, and about 1762 Acadia was invaded, its peaceful inhabitants forcibly removed from their homes.

Many were sent in ships to New Orleans where their descendants are known as "Cajuns," meaning "Canadians." Others fled to New England, some by way of the Great Lakes and familiar river systems. Rivers to the Acadians in reality were like highways to us today. Many early French settlements, such as that at Dayton, border rivers.

So Anna tells us how her ancestors fled via the St. John River, eventually living near Madawaska, (Maine and) New Brunswick, where Hubert was born. She speaks of her "one thousand cousins" back in New Brunswick and in New England, so we can begin to trace their routes west to Minnesota. Magloire DeMars came before 1850 to the Minnesota Territory, working his way up the Mississippi to the Itasca and Dayton area. He had lived in one of the dozen or so first tiny houses of early Pig's Eye (later called St. Paul) and drove wagons for Louis Robert in the area. A bridge and a major St. Paul street named for Robert today cross the Mississippi between downtown St. Paul and West St. Paul.

Magloire found temporary housing in what is now Dayton in the historic Goodin home, one of many first comers who passed their earliest days there. His daughter Adeline ("Adele"), born in Dayton in 1860, married Hubert Fournier twenty years later, whose family had also settled early on in Dayton.

Ma's oldest brother Brazell DeMars, born in the Dayton/Rogers area, traveled with his own oxcarts between the 1870s and about 1905, by the old Red River trails between Pembina (now in North Dakota) near the Canadian and Minnesota border, and Dayton. Along with other settlers, he sometimes traveled from Fort Snelling up the Minnesota River, fording to the Red River and thence northward down the Red.

By contrast we see reflected in Anna's letters, Laurence Dare, son, grandson and great-grandson of early Orono settlers. The families originated in England, France and Wales by way of many early Puritans and pilgrims to America in the very same years as Anna's French ancestors landed not far north of Plymouth, forming Acadia.

LAD's grandparents on both sides had come to Elk River in the 1860s and early 1870s, lived and died here. They were all of protestant heritage. His mother, (Susan) "May" Albee Dare and family were busy in the W.C.T.U. and united against all alcohol, although this seemed to form a barrier between them and other European immigrants. It was also true that neither Ma nor Anna approved of such consumption. This proved a factor in Anna's favor with respect to the family of LAD.

Laurence's father was Arthur Newman Dare who had combined two local newspapers about 1880 into the Sherburne County Star News. He was its first editor and publisher. Laurence became the second, and his son Charles Fournier Dare, my husband, was the third.

In the attic of our home on Main Street, which Arthur was building in 1880, I have learned far more about the ancestry of my husband and our daughter, Jenny Sue, than all the facts told me by the family to date. In one of hundreds of letters to May Dare, saved in the attic before 1900, is mentioned the family's private nickname for the Star News: it was known as the GFJ, or the "Great Family Journal."

I also learned the reference to the house they built and in which we now live as "The Dare Mansion." I hadn't realized that while Arthur worked in the state capitol between 1903 and 1907, the Dares had moved to St. Paul when Arthur (or AND) was State Printer after representing Sherburne County for three terms in the state legislature, the last as speaker. The three St. Paul residences were therefore known as "The Dare Mansion," in their turn.

My hope in publishing these letters for the public is that the reader will encounter interesting aspects of life in Elk River and Otsego nearly a hundred years ago, and meet the writer, Anna, and her neighbors, classmates, teachers and family in a way which heightens the communities' sense of their past. In meeting LAD and Anna in this personal way, we see our similarities, and how things have changed (such as high school) and some of us look back literally to our own ancestors. I've found that the more we recognize our personal and community histories, the more personal history becomes.

As an adopted child, I had a mother, Jennie, who cared for me, taught me and met my child needs. Years after she passed away, I learned that my birth mother likewise wanted to meet me. With professional help I at last met Ann and my three half-sisters, Becky, Pat and Mary Lou, who all mean a great deal to me.

When I married Charlie, I had a stepmother-in-law, Rose. Still I longed to learn and share with my husband more about his mother. Anna had died unexpectedly, leaving three young children. Charlie, who was only three and a half, has no memory of her, nor does his sister Donna Mary who was just seven months old. Their brother Alan, at 11, remembered her clearly, and was old enough to experience a powerful sense of grief and loss to the day of his own death on December 17, 2002, at age 87.

Now it's my delight to share what I've learned from the letters in the attic about the special woman who has become my "other" mother.

Laurence Albee Dare

Anna Delia Fournier

Letters before the Bridge

1903-1907

July 23, 1903

Laurence Dear,

I'll bet you've been wondering night and day if I got your letter. I wasn't at home when it came but I got it alright. Mr. Staples the postman was mighty anxious to see who was going after it.

We're going to have the biggest company! They are my aunts and uncles, Mr. and Mrs. Brazell DeMars of Bathgate, N.D., and Mr. and Mrs. Nazareth Chevalier of Benson, Minnesota. But they will stay a month, so I'll have plenty of time to see them.

I didn't think you'd miss the "dear Laurence." I didn't like it a little bit when you said I was a "dear." Perhaps I am but I don't want to know it. Well, I won't be "sassy" any more. Don't worry about Mathias. He goes with another pretty girl.

Sakes alive! An automobile went by this afternoon. It went like the wind.

Goodbye,
Anna

July 25, 1903

Laurence Dear,

I can't wait for you until three o'clock 'cause if you don't come, I'll go to Grandpa's. Yes, Ma thinks I could go alone with you, but it wouldn't be as nice as if we were several. If you aren't here by one or one-thirty, I shall leave at that time.

Don't bother about what "Ma chere" means. Did you get that out of some novel?

Ma chere *means "Dear one;" French feminine.*

Goodbye,
Anna

Left to right: Benoit, Anna & Joseph Fournier (about 1902-1905)

August 8, 1903

Laurence Dear,

I was very glad to get your letter. Land, I can eat many more bananas than that. One time when I went to Minneapolis I ate seven without stopping. You ought to have stayed and eaten that bunch.

Ma doesn't want me to read another book, 'cause if I start a book I read the whole time and neglect my music shamefully.

I was so mad at myself! I didn't tell you I had a nice time last Sunday. You went away before I could think of it. It was a delightful drive and I enjoyed it immensely. What would you have done if I had left my jacket in the buggy? I came very near forgetting it.

Our ferryman Mr. Vassar has bought a new farm. Only forty acres, but land out here is so rich and valuable that he can easily make a living on forty acres.

Lightning struck Mr. Chouinard's house last Tuesday morning. Hurt Mr. C's arm awfully and knocked one of the boys over and he has been awfully sick. A narrow escape, wasn't it?

Dear! Dear! The Ladies Aid Society has asked me to speak to the supper in the Otsego Methodist Episcopal church next Tuesday and I don't see how I am going to get out of it. They're bound that I should go. Wouldn't you like to go to the supper? Don't suppose your ma will let you. It's to make money for church.

Goodbye Laurie,
A.D.F.

August 13, 1903

Dear Laurence,

Yes, there's a ferry there, but there may be a bridge before long. Much better.

I should be greatly pleased to be presented with one of your cards.

Although it is very late, I feel in duty bound to answer your note. Papa began to tell us about our ancestors and, though it was the hundredth time I had heard it told, I was so interested that I couldn't get away. You didn't know that I was Acadian from the Basin of Minns, did you? I am. Read Evangeline again to learn what good people they were.

I should think it would be lonesome at home now that Susan and Mrs. Dare have gone to St. Paul. Bennie is away this evening and we miss the dear little one so. He is the baby, but though he is nine, we care more for him than others.

Dear me! I hope you'll give me a ride when you get your automobile. Never rode in one. I think I must be the blundering idiot 'cause I never noticed that you didn't act as a gentleman should. I'd give anything to hear you sing.

Catch many fish? I got poison ivy down back of your house yesterday. My face is on fire. Poison ivy is horrible stuff. I have it every summer.

Awful lonesome here in the country! Still, it isn't bad —I read and write a great deal, and nearly all of the girls write often and come to see me occasionally. The piano and bicycle are lots of company also.

Goodbye,
Anna

August 19, 1903

Dear Laurence,

I wouldn't sit on that second seat if Miss Dunn said I had to. No sir, not I, after she has made me sit on the front seat. Wicked to skip when you have three recitations in the afternoon. I like to have figures on the black board.

I love to look at you, you're so pretty. I walk up with Carl nearly every morning. Are you jealous?? Ha! Ha! I am teaching him to scrap and he isn't a very apt pupil. He always agrees with me.

It will be all right for L.A.D. to go to St.Paul and enjoy himself, if there is no harm involved. He knows what that means. No thinking seriously of any girl, but friendly, kind and respectful to all. Also if he will go to church mornings and remember it is the Sabbath day, and not to be spent like a week day in excursions. This once because Anna Delia loves him and he cannot refuse, when so politely asked.

Yes the roads over there are pretty good and I know the way out there. Try to get a double buggy. That would be so much nicer. If it wasn't at night I could have our rig.

Anna

August 26, 1903

Laurie Dear,

Yes, dear, you may come over to see me next Thursday evening at whatever time will suit you best. I'll be out on the porch. Sure! Oh, let me tell you something. Last Saturday (I think) Pa was in the tailor shop looking at the suits and things. He wants to get a new suit. Ma asked him what there was there and what he liked best. He said, "There is one piece that has a bluish tint in it that I liked better than all the rest."

I declared I bet it was like Laurie's. I said it was dark blue. "Yes," he says, "I'll bet it was; it's a fine piece of goods."

Is Carl's suit something like yours? My black suit only cost $19.38. That is for the whole suit; hat, shoes and dress. My white suit cost $13.37. Pa doesn't mind getting me nice clothes 'cause I wear them so long. I have worn my white suit for two years and intend to wear it for two more years without washing it once. You know that I wore it rain or shine, through mud and water to the C.M.A. party, Senior Reception, Fourth of July, etc.

Pa, Ma and I took a dandy walk in the woods last Sunday. We found some fine plums.

Pa told us a lot about farming and it was interesting. Pa says he never heard of that poem Evangeline, about the Acadians and the English taking them away. He tells an altogether different story, 'cause his folks didn't stay to be taken away. They fled up the St. John River! It's awfully interesting, more so than Evangeline 'cause we know that Pa's story is true and it's about our ancestors.

Pa's great grandfather was three months old when the folks moved to New Brunswick. This story was handed down from father to son until it has come to us. (It was mother to son in Pa's case.) Grandpa died when Pa was only six years old.

I'll tell you all that story sometime. It's too much work to write it out. Sometime before I die I intend to go out there and find out more from my old uncles and relatives. Pa is going next winter. So is Ma. Won't we be lonesome with only a hired girl and a hired man? I'm dying to go.

Ma is going to Anoka tomorrow and I'll have to stay alone all day. I'm pretty scared.

I had a fine ride on the new plow. I put my foot on a thing I didn't know about and left the thing down on Joe's foot. I love to work with horses.

Goodbye,
"Nanny goo" or "Old Nan"

September 9, 1903

Dear Laurie,

"The day is cold and dark and dreary.
It rains and the wind is ever weary."

I got ready for church, and then I didn't go. I slept
half the day and made candy and I got my feet wet,
and now my knee that I hurt in "runaway" aches and
everything is horrid when it rains.

I must tell you how people are using me. Leon loans
me his "keen kutter," but he won't translate German
for me. He gave me one of his cards, so I forgave him.
It's awfully cute.

Freddie treated me, so he's O.K. Carl doesn't tease
me; very good. Shirley Mills keeps still, is so oblig-
ing. Harold shouts, "L.A.D.," at me in the street. Arthur
sympathizes. Charles doesn't say much. Did you think
he would be likely to?

But Leslie!!!! He was to come to see me this afternoon but it rained. He tries to kill flies that are crawl-
ing on my waist, right in school, too. He jabs his pencil into me and is forever doing something. I nearly
had a fight with him Friday. I asked if he could sit still
one minute. He told me to "shut up." I was very much
offended and told him that wasn't a very gentlemanly
remark, and there would be trouble if he said it again.
I haven't spoken to him since, and don't mean to until
he apologizes.

Tell that girl next door to you that she need not be
nice to you 'cause I'm prettier than she is, see?

I'd never heard the last of it if I had seen you off on
the train. The kids would have made out that I cried.
The ferryman is the only sensible fellow. Never said a
word.

Yes, I did care. I'm glad you're better mannered than
some boys. I thought that was all you'd learned in those

*A cutter is a
small, light sleigh
usually pulled
by one horse.*

French novels. I suppose I'll have to be very good to
you now that you're away. My! You must be lonesome
when you have never lived anywhere but in Elk River.
I am getting along famously (!!) in school. Charles
Houlton and I are the smartest kids in History. Miss
Van makes Literature easy for us little fellows and I
can explain poetry just fine. Second German isn't any-
thing like First. Miss Dunn calls us Frauleins Fournier,
Moores, Beck, Davis and Whitman. Small class. Herr
Libby will join us after Christmas.

*Peril in the
biology lab*

I have twenty-five specimens already. I'm having
an awful time with them. My chloroform isn't good
and they just go to sleep. When I lift the cover they are
all wiggling. Finally, I got mad, took a fine big black
bug and stuck his head in the liquid and he got so stiff
that his legs all broke off and I couldn't do anything
with him. After I close my eyes at night, all I can see is
a profusion of wings, legs and antennae all kicking
about like a regular cyclone. Awful!

Oh, I kill the frog before I cut its heart out.

Goodbye,
Anna

September 14, 1903

Laurie Dear,

I guess I'll write you a little piece before I go to studying.

It's raining "pitchforks and barn shovels." Lightning! Thunder!! I've got my hair done up nice and I have a pleasant smile on my face, so if I die, I won't be likely to look hideous. My room and desk are in order and there isn't a single scrap of paper near my seat at school, so people would say I was awfully neat. See?

I saw Laura Bailey (Leslie's sister) and Miss Dare this evening. It was the first time I had seen Laura since the C.M.A. party, but she knew me from clear across the street. She was driving that wonderful horse. Is she anything like Leslie? By the way, Leslie and I had a foot fight today. I won; he was scared.

Joe's been up here studying and I didn't write then, so now I've forgotten what I was going to say. I've awful times with him. He finds so much to attract his attention up here that he doesn't study and keeps asking me what this paper is for, why is that card there.

Goodbye,
Anna D.F.

September 21, 1903

Dear Laurence,

I nearly fell over when I got your letter, I was so surprised. It was very welcome, though.

There was a buyer here last Saturday and I began to weep when I saw him. He liked the farm so well, and he didn't think $12,000 was too much for it. Oh, dear! I couldn't bear to leave.

I slapped Nuttie's face, fair and square, last Friday. You probably heard his story. Dan threw a huge piece of crayon clear across the room and hit a whack, plump on my cheek. In a second it was swollen as big as the whole end of my little finger.

I can't sing quite as high as that, but I can screech it! Just then I saw you come and I thought you were coming to school. I started toward the cloak room door and yelled at him, "You hurt me just awful; there, a big bump there; and Laurence is going to see it! Boo-hoo-hoo!!"

Just then, Mr. Norval came in and said, "Laurence isn't coming here, he's gone through the woods."

Goodbye,
Anna

October 15, 1903

Dear Laurence,

Yes, I have that song now, and it's awfully pretty and easy to play. Land, that man must have thought you were mighty little to be married. I am simply dying for an opal ring, but I can't hope ever to get it until I earn it.

I asked Freddie why he told you that story, and he said he wanted to know how often you wrote. "I judge that he writes at least once a week," he says.

You need not hurt Leslie a bit 'cause he always gets the worst every time. We fight every day. Our worst fight was last Monday. As I said before, he is forever jabbing his pencil into me. Well, I turned around and it rather surprised him that I tried to hit him. He actually said, "Gaul darn you."

Why! I was so mad! I wanted to fly at him but I was scared of Miss D, so I wrote a note to him:

Leslie,
I don't think it was a bit smart or cute either, the way you spoke to me this morning. I can forgive most anything but I can't have anything to do with anyone who is rude or impolite. So you need not speak to me until you can be a gentleman.
Anna.

He showed it to the boys and had a big time but I wasn't going to have him make a fool of me. He thought it over a while and it was mighty serious. Finally, he wrote: "I am very sorry I can't fill L.A.D.'s place, aren't you? L.D.B."

I never answered. At noon he waited until the lines had passed and he walked up to me and said, "What are we going to do about it?" I told him; and at noon he came in and asked me about History and was angelic.

"Nanny Goo" is Joe's name for me. You must hunt up some nice name for yourself. I won't call you "punkin" anymore but I can call you Laurie, can't I?

About fifteen boys came to take me to the dance the other night, but it was a school night. Compliments? "Why, Anna, you look like a big red rose of summer." Nice!

Joe Libby tells things awfully funny in Literature. I never knew him before. The other day I asked him if he had outlined Vicar of Wakefield. He says, "No! I read about nineteen pages and was so lovesick I couldn't get farther." Shocking?

The morning after you came, I wasn't very nice to L.D.B. He says, "What happened to you last night? Laurence was awful cranky this morning and here you are about to eat me up."

The Dares had two horses, Starlight and Starbright.

He says he is tired of feeding your horse Star Light and there's a big bumblebee's nest in the cutter. Today he asked me if my initials were A.D.F. He says he got a letter from you, and "A.D.F." was scribbled all over the paper. He's a punkin. I told him my initials were X.Y.Z.

I weigh the least of any girl in High School. Lucile weighs fifteen pounds more than I. So would you believe it! One hundred and one pounds.

Mrs. Upham died while talking over the phone Thursday evening. Her last words were, "Is this Mrs. White?"

Isn't that awful? Dan told me.

Goodbye,
Anna

October 28, 1903

Laurence Dear,

This is Saturday evening and I've just gotten home. I'm so tired but I want to write now so I can tell you about my visit, and not omit a single detail.

Well, to begin with, we girls have organized a glee club and we meet every other Friday evening. There's Mabel, Cecil, Lucile, Silly, Bessie, Blanche and me. And we invited George, Fred, Carl, Dan, Willie, Leslie and Joe L.

We met at Hindley's last night and Bessie couldn't go, and I don't know why Leslie didn't go. We had an oyster stew, salad, cake and apples, and it was simply fine. Oh, the table was so prettily decorated with branches of prickly ash and bittersweet berries.

Rev. Hindley was the pastor of Union Church.

When Lucile invited Leslie he didn't know whether he could go or not: "How much do you want?"

Lucile says, "We're making the party and we don't want anything."

"Well, perhaps I can go then, if it won't cost me anything." But he wasn't there. After supper the boys practiced signals and we washed the dishes. When they came back we marched, sang, played "Pig in the Parlor," and whistled; Blanche sang soprano, Lucille Hindley, also. First time I ever played on the piano in a crowd. I didn't do it bad, though, so don't worry.

Joe Libby is a circus. Mrs. Hindley played an awful lot for us. They sang some awfully pretty songs. We came home at 11:30. Cecil and Dan took me home. Dan gave us each a ticket to go to the football game.

Every young one I came in contact with calls me "Aunty." Liddie's children when they saw me come, began to call, "Voila' ma tante," and Eleanor Corey calls me "Aunty." Her father asked her who that girl was and she said, "She's my Aunty." Liddy has two children and her sister was visiting her and she had

Means "There's my Aunt" in French.

three, and there were two at Corey's. I never kissed so many dirty faces in all my life. I got acquainted with an awfully nice girl today, Ruth Atkins.

What do you think Leslie said to me the other day? He said, "Say, Anna, Laurence has a girl down in St. Paul, so you might as well go with me." I asked him what he took me for.

Lucile said she saw you, and you put her things on the train for her. Leslie took the liberty to put my back comb in straight 'cause he "wanted me to look pretty," he said.

I'm so glad you're coming back to Elk River to stay. I'm going to a party next Saturday given by the freshman class on Halloween. When they organized, President Wheaton wrote on the board,

"Meeting of Fresherman Class Tonight."

The man who wrote Under the Bamboo Tree must have liked geometry. "Things equal to the same thing are equal to each other."

It was pitch dark when I came home, and I was scared half to death. But Leon happened to be down at the ferry, so he rode my wheel home and I went home with his sisters by horse and buggy. Wasn't he angelic?

We're going to have a furnace as soon as we get the 'taters out of the cellar.

Goodbye,
Anna Delia

P.S. Leslie thinks my name is Dil-i-a. We scrap continuously.

A "wheel" is a bicycle.

November 16, 1903

Dear Laurence,

Last Saturday at this time we were at the dance, November 14. I'm invited out to dinner at Mrs. Herrick's for tomorrow noon. She wrote and told me that if I had a gentleman friend, she extended the invitation to him also. I answered and said that my gentleman friend regretted that it was impossible for him to accept. I'm going alone, though.

To tell the truth, Laurence, I can't remember to save me if I thought of you when I had my picture taken. I know I thought how cold and red and swollen my nose must look. On the other negative, my mouth was enormous because Bessie made me laugh. On this one I straightened my mouth after he had taken it. Lucky for you that you did take Cecilia's 'cause that was the only way you could get me to give you one.

Oh, Land, don't worry about Dan. Yes, I'm positive. You know how I used to ring the school bell for him? Well, Monday noon, if you were still in Elk River you probably heard it. Dear!!

"Dan, Dan, Dan, something's the matter with that bell!! It won't ring and I've got about a mile of rope down here." Dan called Carl to help him turn the bell over. Everyone is telling about my strength.

That same night I dreamt that I fell off the ferry boat and called for Leon the same as I had called to Dan. It was awful!

Did your ma jaw you? Honest, I forgot you had promised her. I'm awfully sorry. Tell her it was all my fault. I remember you hesitated before going in. Why didn't you remind me!

You can't imagine how I love to dance. Skating next. I'll never do it again. I'm a thoughtless wretch anyway. I don't suppose your mother can ever forgive me? I never thought of your promise.

Carl had Mabel with him then. Carl goes with that new Johnson girl. He took her home from church last Sunday. Again from downtown last night. She is only thirteen years old. My, I hope you'll come before next spring. I looked for you at school Monday; Joe said he saw you, but I didn't.

Goodbye,
Anna

"La Petite" in French.

P.S. Seems funny to hear you call me "Little Girl." No one but Pa, Ma, and kids ever call me that.

November 24, 1903

Dear Laurence,

Oh, Land! If you want that long a letter, I'll have to begin to write it now. We get our mail in the morning now. It's kind of lonesome not to have to look for the mailman at night.

The river is frozen over above and below the ferry and it's all open at the crossing. We'll probably have to cross with the boat the greater part of the winter, unless the ice goes out again this fall.

I stayed over two days with Cecile the first night I came home; the young folks skated on the pond. I haven't skated for two years.

Last Tuesday morning the anchor ice was running awfully thick and Vassar didn't want to take me across because it was dangerous. But I finally persuaded him to take me over. We went up as far as the pier and tried to go across in an open place. We got halfway over and that channel ended so we had to turn back and rowed for shore.

Then we saw a nice open place. We hadn't gone over ten feet when the ice closed in all around us and we couldn't do a thing, except float down with the ice. We had to keep the boat rocking to keep it from getting frozen solid. It was awfully cold in the middle of the river and there was some pretty cold ice in the bottom of the boat to keep your feet warm with. We just calmly sat there for about three quarters of an hour floating down stream.

Dangers of crossing the river.

Burt Carr, who happened to be caught on our side of the river, wanted to take off his fur coat and let me have it but I declared I wasn't very cold. Gracious Heavens!

Finally, when we had reached the rapids, the ice happened to break away just where we were, and we started back for our shore. But I was determined to go to school! Just then there was a channel clear across that blessed river (I saw it too!) and Vassar rowed with all his might; we got there just in time before it closed around us again. It was very thrilling; cold, too.

Oh, that wasn't the funniest part of it. We couldn't get landed 'cause it was so shallow, the boat struck the rocks in the bottom of the river. Joe stepped on the ice near the shore and dragged the boat so that I could step out. Joe ran so fast that by the time Mr. Carr and I were ready to start, he was far out of sight.

It struck me awfully funny when he and I ran side by side clear uptown, about a mile, only stopped to crawl under fences and over logs and thru willow groves. He could hardly run with his coat and my dinner box under his arm. Anyone would have died laughing to see us.

I might have told this in a more interesting manner, but honest, I shiver now when I think of it. Vassar and Mr. Carr said I ought to get high marks in school and get credit for my wonderful courage. If that man hadn't been with me, I'd have broken plump down and cried.

I do that very easily anyway. So, I'm not so courageous after all. I was late, but Miss Dunn excused me and was glad I was able to get to school at all. The boys didn't dare to go over. I wasn't a bit scared, but I didn't care much for a watery grave in that "frigidus" dress.

Goodnight,
Anna Delia

A letter from Nettie Thomas

November 26, 1904

My Dear Anna,

Will try and write a letter now and finish it after German.

I am so awfully sorry you are indisposed; hope you will be able to come tomorrow. I have oceans of things to tell you.

Miss Dunn favored us with a few minute lecture this A.M. As a result everyone who crosses the threshold for any reason whatsoever without putting his name on the board will be suspended for not less than two weeks!

She gave us various other pointers about the different "spirits" which pervade the school, and about the "spirit" of lawlessness in particular. Mr. Stahl followed her worthy example and "harangued" for five minutes this afternoon.

Miss Churchill is all together too good to be classed with such "cross- patches" as Miss D and Mr. S; just think, she actually read us a story that took up the whole recitation period!

Nettie

November 28, 1903

"Father of Waters" is the Mississippi River.

I went skating on the Father of Waters this afternoon. I skated about fifteen minutes and was so tired I had to come home. Maybe the boys weren't perfectly delighted to get me out! I never saw them so angelic. They carried my skates and wanted to take me down there in their wagon.

I was surprised to find what a poor skater I was. I go about half a rod, then I sit down and rest five minutes. Mamma thinks I skate gracefully.

I tell you, I'm getting so many compliments lately that I'm almost ashamed of myself. Last Sunday Mrs. Herrick said I looked like a little fairy when I wore my pussy hood. I'm the only mortal that wears one. Even the little ones don't wear those hoods.

A pussy hood was a close fitting, warm winter hat or bonnet, tied by strings under the chin. It was often gray and soft, resembling the short fur on a cat's head.

Jennie Lefebvre said that I was a quiet girl and not a bit talkative, but I make things pleasant for everyone around me. Wouldn't that knock you?

Leslie and I scrap continually as usual. He's the only boy in his family and I'm the only girl in mine, so naturally we're both spoiled. Mamma says that he is just as much of a baby as I am. He doesn't like to have me tell Ma everything, so we had a bigger scrap than ever last Friday. I wrote an awful note to him and he laughed right out loud. It tickled me so. I turned around and said, "Leslie, I'll slap your face."

I thought he'd tell me to shut up. Instead of that he said, "Oh, no, don't!" He said it so funny, too; just as tho' he'd said it to a little child.

It struck him funny the other day when Cecilia and I wore each other's waists. They were simply perfect. Cecilia looked smaller and I looked larger, so we both looked better than with our own.

A.D.F.

December 1, 1903

Poor Laurence,

You pumpkin (beg pard), why do you always look at me when I look at the black board. Every time I look up, you are looking at me. What happened—you said you couldn't sit with me any more. Why are you not allowed? Do your folks object?

You appoint a trysting place and then you don't tryst (that's Greek to me). But you did. Yas.

A "trysting place" is a meeting place.

That is funny that you made that mistake. Last winter my cousin wrote two letters to some pretty nice girls and put the letters in the wrong envelopes. When I got the blank letter, I thought that you wanted to end our correspondence and had taken this means of telling me. Mighty lucky that you found the old note 'cause I wasn't going to write again.

I guess it does you good to work if you have gained seven pounds. I have been working hard, too. Last week Pa broke his binder and as usual I had to do housework while Ma was out trying to comfort him and convince him that it wouldn't rain, etc. Dear! I built every load of hay for three days. Uncle Fred said I did it well, too. I sprained my wrist. We had a runaway, but the work went on regardless. I take great pleasure in milking three cows every Sunday morning and evening.

A farm girl's chores.

I can't go to the city before next summer, that is, to visit.

That farmer DeMarse is my uncle Brazell, Ma's brother. I guess his wife won't stop here on her way back from New England when she hears of this misfortune. We got a letter from their family. They make it much worse than that. Many logs were burned, every carriage and buggy burned, all their sheds were burned to the ground. The house would have followed if it hadn't been raining so hard. Every pane of glass on one side of the house was broken.

I don't mind telling you who took me to the dance. Ma took me to Dayton and then I went to the hall with my cousin and Walter Kirk, the young man with whom Lori Sophia has been going. I had supper and came home with them, too. Wasn't I good!

I wouldn't read so many French novels if I were you.

Goodbye,
Anna

December 4, 1903

Dear Laurence,

I cross upriver at Mr. Gray's now. I ride a mile and walk two. I told Papa I'd rather earn that fifty cents a week than give it to Vassar. We can't cross with teams yet. The ice is awfully thin near the shore, so we walk on boards. Oh, it's so slippery. I protect my nose with my muff. Joe goes ahead of me and fairly drags me along, carries my things too, good? It isn't dangerous, except that we're liable to fall in any minute. I ain't scared. The water wouldn't be over our heads there.

You know the cattle that escaped from the train wreck? Well, one of those fellows came down to our house, and went straight to the barnyard gate to go in with our stock. Then some men came and shot him. They had chased him from Big Lake. He crossed the river at Mr. Cooley's.

Ya, wohl, I would enjoy going to Minneapolis every week. Why, of course, I was perfectly delighted to meet Mr. Dare in the depot. I was dying to see you. I was so tickled I nearly fainted. Didn't you notice how my hands trembled? A perfectly glorious time!

Yup! I guess we are very good friends. That song is lovely. I never heard "Little Gurly Gurl." No, I don't mind being called "Little Girl." That's what Ma calls me more than half the time. In French, she calls me "La Petite", which means "Little One."

That's so, we've never had a quarrel. Not even a scrap because you never disagree, and let me have my way. But I have a world wide reputation of being mighty cranky. Ask Vassar.

No, I wasn't angry with you for making me ride in the elevator. I suppose I would have been awfully tired walking; I thought it would make me dizzy and sick; to ride three or four stories isn't bad but it nearly kills me. Glorification! Fourteen stories! But that elevator

Elevator ride in Minneapolis.

wasn't like those in the stores. Nevertheless, I had a constant desire to hang on to the sides. I was afraid to smash my fingers. No, I never went so near Heaven before. Wonderful!

There's a little snow on the ground. Not deep enough for a sleigh, but just enough for me to wade knee deep in.

The boys said it took me twenty minutes to read your letter. "Look at the stack of paper," they exclaimed. I was keeping house that night.

"Sister'd be cranky if she didn't get a letter."

Can you?

I wish I was your cousin or relative to get a picture for Christmas. You wouldn't want my picture in your watch cover. Yes, they do tease me occasionally, tho' not near as much. I can't imagine what "G.B.M.D.C.Y.K.B.M." means. Tell me!

The rooster crowed at about 9:30 the other evening. Means death in the family. Don't be surprised if you don't get a letter because I may die of chicken pox.

Goodbye,
Anna

December 7, 1903

Laurie,

This evening Ma was looking at Bennie and she said, "Ben is going to look just like Papa."

"Oh, Mamma, please don't make me think of it," he says. That young one is as vain as a girl. He looks at himself in the glass for hours when he is dressed up. He lacks some gloves, and his eyes are sore. He lacks glasses. He's worse than I am. The boys were laughing at you this evening because you didn't know about a basement in a barn, but insisted on putting your horse up where we keep all the hay and grain. Hope you'll know next time, so they won't tease me so much. We have a fine (!!) swing there in the summertime.

Goodbye, I've changed my name to
Anna Delia Fournier

P.S. Be sure to tell me where my picture is. Yours is stuck in the corner of the large mirror in my room.

I forgot to tell you I went to a "Book Social" last week. I wore paper girls cut from a catalog and I was "Little Women." Cecilia wore the same, just exactly the same. But she was "Wee Girls." Laura Bailey was there and she had little girls. I asked her if she wasn't "Wee Girls." Then of course she guessed Cecilia's.

The lady is going to Minneapolis on the early train and coming back on the early train Friday. If you want to see me, I'll be at the depot in the afternoon. Mama said I could go to Monticello if I wanted to but I don't know if she'd let me go alone with a boy. Couldn't you get a two-seated buggy and go two couples? We might take a lunch and have a big time.

A bit of whimsy written by Anna in 1903

A Story of Ye Olden Time
By Anna Fournier

In these modern times, in 1975, one can hardly believe such strange things could happen as I am about to relate. But times have changed the aspect of things and, in the year 1903, one had to take his chances of fording a stream or depending on a ferry.

In those days, what is now the great city of Elk River, was nothing but a struggling village which had much ado to keep its very name alive. The town had been trying for some time to obtain a bridge across the Mississippi in that place, but had so far been unsuccessful and still depended on the old leaky ferry. To get down to my story, a boys' club or society, the C.M.A. of Elk River, had planned to give a party. When the day arrived, rain was falling and this kept up continually, but the boys decided it was too late to postpone their party and so it came off. A goodly assembly of lads and lassies were there. They were entertained right royally.

At midnight, the guests began to leave the hall. It was the darkest night ever known in that section of the country and not a street lamp was lighted.

One of the young ladies who had attended the party was a Miss Anna Fournier, by name, whose home was about a mile across the river. Her mother had planned to meet her at the opposite side, but oh! How terrible are the fates!

A young man named Laurence A. Dare, the son of a prominent statesman, gallantly gave Miss Fournier his arm to escort her to the other side of the river. It was intensely dark, but the two managed to find their way to the old ferry bell which she rang to summon the ferry man. They then proceeded down to the river which at this point had worn away the bank so that it was a sort of a precipice.

On account of the darkness they could not see a foot ahead of them and they unconsciously stepped off the bank into the whirling eddy below. The ferryman heard their cries for help and quickly came over and received the now unconscious maiden from the arms of the youth; she was now safe from the terrible waters. But not so the lad, who after his heroic efforts in saving the girl, had sunk back, never to rise again. A monument in honor of the gallant boy was erected on the banks of the old Mississippi, which alone can account for the untimely loss of this bright lad who was just entering upon a life of sunshine and joy.

As to the maiden, she will long be remembered as one of the greatest women in the work of charity and help for the poor. That name was always the same: Miss Anna Fournier

January 15, 1904

Dear Laurence.

Leslie stole one of my curls and he's going to send it to you.

I studied until one A.M. last Sunday and until eleven last night. I'm going to take five subjects the last half. I don't know if I can stand it, but if I can't I'll have to stand being sick, 'cause I won't give up.

I'm going to stay a couple of days with Ruth soon. Ma is making me an awfully pretty dressing sac. Pale yellow dotted Swiss. I'm going to have another one just like Mrs. Romdenne's. White lawn with pink polka dots in it. I'll wear it when you come if you'll wear your white sweater.

I can't make these two statements coincide: "Write a long letter, if you have to sit up all night," and "Don't let your beauty be marred by late hours." Can you?

Sentimental? You are sentiment personified. I sent Miss Brown much love yesterday. Did you want me to tell her you sent yours? My cousin wants me to send her your picture. Shall I? She must think lots of the boy she goes with.

I was mean to Bennie tonight. I persuaded Ma not to let him read at night, so I wouldn't have to have him in my room while I was writing to you. I'll be extra ordinarily good some other time to make up.

Goodbye,
Anna

January 22, 1904

Dear Laurence,

No, I don't graduate until next year. I may graduate in Little Falls. We refused $10,000 for our farm last Saturday. We'd take $12,000. Lord! I'd die! I wouldn't see you very often then. Save us!

If you knew what I thought of your picture, you wouldn't say that. My cousin only wanted to see it because I told her you were handsome. I look at it by the hour and think lots of it.

I'm going to be in the play MacBeth. I'm an old witch dressed in gray mosquito netting and talk in a low tone. I didn't know my voice was naturally low. C.E.D. said it was: "Her voice is low and sweet."

Don't say anything about that curl to Leslie because he'll think I'm an awful girl. I'll give you one if you won't tell him. Before I retire I always curl my hair around my face so that if I die during the night, I'd look pretty, and Ma can cut them and give them away. Aren't I funny?

What made you think that I didn't care for you? I thought I had showed you too many times that I did. Don't you like Ruth Atkins? I do. She does me. Bessie said so.

My Dear Dare is going to take me to the dance. It isn't every boy that would want to be a substitute. Carl takes Bessie, so I expect Leslie will take Laura. It's a senior dance Friday night.

You like Miss Dunn? She told Letitia and me, "Just because I like you two girls you needn't think that you can do anything the other pupils can't do!" Wouldn't that knock you!

I'm anxious to see your diary and book of accounts. You needn't think I believed you when you said there was "no love in your home." There is in every home.

Pa worked for the Mississippi and Rum River Boom Company as far away as Little Falls and Brainerd, Minnesota.

A girl that has half a grain of principle about her will never show how much she cares for a boy, because then if he doesn't care for her, she'll be talked of like hundreds of others.

I didn't think you and I would ever quarrel after we'd gotten along so nicely for nearly a year; broken record. Oh, I wish I had two hearts so you could have one and the rest of humanity could share the other. But as it is, you can't have it all.

Did you read Hoher als die Kirche in German? It's an awful love story and the girl is just awful. She lets that boy kiss her anytime he wants to and she never objects. Miss D said she would get some History for us to read; she didn't know that it would create such a sensation in the class. Yesterday L.D.B. had to stand by the waste box and tear up paper half the night.

Goodbye.
Anna D.F.

January 23, 1904

Blanche R., Lucile Hindley, one other girl and I are going to act out a song, dressed in white cheesecloth and our hair fixed pretty. Won't that be nice? You must come and see what a good actress I can be. So graceful and pretty.

Oh, dear, I'm going to be a pretty girl and a horrid witch the same night! I'm this witch. Ever read MacBeth? I don't know when it's going to be.

This morning L.D.B. called me up the stairs like a puppy, snapping his fingers and whistling. This noon he asked Mabel M. who he was going to be in the play and she said, "Jack." It struck me that nearly every dog is named Jack. So I turned around and called, "Jack," and whistled and snapped my fingers, right in school. I was bound I'd get it back on him. He knows what I think of him.

I came near getting drowned this morning. Joe drove me across the river on a hand sled. He went so near the edge of the water that the ice began to crack and crack and I rolled off. My heart stopped beating, and then it beat so fast again. Breathless.

Grandpa and Ma have ninety-four descendants; seventy are living. Eleven children, about seventy-five grand kinder, eight great grand children, two children dead, about twenty grandchildren dead.

Well, the lady must study now. Au revoir.

Anna

January 29, 1904

Dear Laurence,

"Mhur-ja" was common slang for murder.

I was very glad to get your letter last night. You forgot to mail it. Mhur-ja.

Yes, I did cry and it isn't the first time I cried for you. I think that the man who said that a woman liked a man all the better if he had a few bad habits must have been wicked and thought that everyone was gone on him.

Yes, it would be splendid if you would commence to smoke and swear. Then you could teach me how and we'd have splendid times together. I'm sure you would enjoy having me do it much more than I'd enjoy having you do it. I'll tell you a little story about it sometime and prove to you that women don't like men for their bad habits. Too long to tell here.

I had a lovely time at the dance. Fred taught me the new three-step and I danced every time except once. I danced five times with Joe Libby. I like to dance with him. Yes, I'm awful glad you're going to learn. I'd love to dance with you.

I love music. Sweet music always makes me feel sad.

"Our sincerest laughter with some pain is fraught,
Our sweetest songs are those that tell of saddest thought."
Shelley

February 1, 1904

One girl you don't like very well told me that she saw you take your mother to church and you were so nice to her. She must think an awful lot of you. A girl you like, I know, said you had a reputation, especially among the older people of being awfully nice.

Union Church in Elk River.

I've taken three subjects for a week now. I told Mr. S. that I never got through my work until midnight and had to drink strong tea to keep me awake. He said I could graduate with 15 credits, but I don't want to.

Pa said if I wore a calico dress when I graduated he'd give me a $25 watch. Grandma is angelic and she likes me so maybe she'll give me one. She likes our family anyway. She calls Papa "our family angel." Not one in the family has a high school education. Several have gone to business college and a few have gone to convent. None to a high school.

Goodnight.
Anna

P.S. Hurry up and come before the crossing gives out. Do you think we can get along without scrapping anymore? Ma will make us quit writing if there's any more of it, I'm afraid, because it makes me crabby and when "Little Girl" is cranky, it makes home life very unpleasant.

February. 8, 1904

Dear Laurence,

    I had a splendid time at the dance. There was a nice crowd. Last time, only a few of us had on white dresses. This time I was the only one that had on black, not a speck of white. The girls thought my black taffeta was a "beauty." Even Freddie thought I looked good in black; black or white for me always. Fred and George are going to give a dance Friday next. But Pa thinks that "la petite" had better rest this time.

Anna Delia Fournier

March 3, 1904

Dear Laurence,

I ought to be studying, but I'm not. Yes, I know, Laurence, it's been a century since last Sunday. Why didn't I see you Tuesday? I saw L.D.B. going to the barn alone and you had gone with him the day before. You came just in time, 'cause there isn't any crossing today.

You were here at this time last Sunday, 6:30.

What was there in the note you sent by Leslie? Fool! He isn't going to tell you he put his arm around me anymore. You ought to see the note I wrote to him. I tell you, I gave him a piece of my mind for once. But it didn't do very much good 'cause he wanted to kiss me the very same night! I don't know why I don't hate him.

Did you see the piece in the paper about the entertainment? Was it you that "looked on with envy?" Didn't Mabel look pretty that night? So did Blanche (so did I). I'd rather let you take a prettier handkerchief than that rag. Ma wished you'd take my handkerchiefs oftener. She said the whole washing smelled good.

Was L.A.D. the unnamed newspaper critic?

Goodnight. Sleepy!
A.D.F.

March 9, 1904

Dear Laurie,

Oh, it's so exciting. There's a man and woman just came in when we were starting for bed. Ma met the woman when she was at the hospital.

She hadn't seen or heard of her since. She made Mamma guess who she was. After five minutes she decided she'd met her there. Eight years makes people change.

My cousin and her babies came with them. They're downstairs now. I wish Ma would call me but I'm afraid she won't. I've never seen the young ones yet, and haven't seen Eliza for over a year. Scared to go down. Guess I'll get the little ones up here and play with them. Dare not go down 'cause they'll make me play the piano and Eliza plays fine. The baby is squalling at present.

Heea! I went. It's ten now and not a lesson have I got. I played piano and Pa played his violin. I got a lunch for them so I guess they think I'm pretty smart. I'm a spoiled baby anyway. Always have been. If there's a piece of cake stolen, if "Little Girl" did it, the boys don't say a word and think it's O.K.

Goodnight

P.S. Mabel Trask said you sang beautifully at Mr. Williams's funeral.

March 13, 1904

Dear Laurence,

A year ago tonight, at just about this time I was getting ready for Lucile and Blanche's poverty party. I looked at my cambric dress that I wore that night and it's so teeny. I didn't suppose I could grow as much as that in one short year. I weigh 111; you know I weighed 115 last fall when I went to Minneapolis.

Oh, it came within an inch—and you would never have entered our parlor but once again. A man offered to give us $10,000 for our place. He wanted it at whatever price we wanted to ask, but the poor man only had $6,000. He has bought Mr. Orton's farm. Everyone pities him. He has a horrible debt of $4,000. Half of the farm isn't worth much and he hasn't any help. Cost him lots. We pay $200 a year for a man and Joe helps like a man.

Orton's farm became the home of the paternal grandparents of Vice President Hubert Humphrey.

I won't tell you about the play 'cause Susan has undoubtedly told you. She played violin beautifully. I wish I could have seen her. Is she coming back next spring? Pa and Ma want Joe to take lessons of her and if she doesn't come, we won't wait, but send him to Anoka now. I wish you would find out before you write again. Papa went just to hear her play. He doesn't care for anything except singing and violin.

There was just that one day, the day I wrote we didn't have a crossing. Going to have a bridge. Mr. Castle is sure we are. Hope so.

One Monday afternoon I was sick during the last period. I could hardly stand up when I went down to the office. Then I got home and Ora, our hired girl, and Ma worked over me until nine. Did you ever have cramps in your arms? Oh, Glory! I thought I was going into nineteen knots.

I'm awfully sorry your father is so sick. He looked awfully bad the last time I saw him. Too bad. I hope I

Arthur may have had a stroke at this time. He recovered well.

won't be sick before Dr. Whittemore gets well. I don't
want another near me. It was bad enough to have him
around when I liked him so well. Someone told us that
he thought the world of our family.

I have a perfect passion for shells, lots of lace, lots
of things to eat, pretty dishes, and fuille curtains. Oh,
and camphor, too. Tons of it.

Goodbye,
Anna

P.S. You got a compliment. Pa saw your sister Susan
Saturday. He said she was pretty and looked an awful
lot like you. See? That's true! You'll have to come next
Sunday if you want to come before your birthday. I
was awfully disappointed when I saw L.D.B. come in
alone last night. I've rubbed my cheeks to pieces and
that red powder won't come off. There's some on every towel and pillow in the house. It hurts. It's all over
my face now.

*Red play
makeup.*

March 25, 1904

No school for a whole week. None today, either. Visiting day.

Now I can sew to my heart's content. I've made half a scarf for my dresser already. I've got twelve new handkerchiefs with lace on 'em, too. I hemstitched a white silk handkerchief for your birthday present, but I don't like to send things through the mail. You'll have to promise me never to let anyone see it before you can have it. It's horribly poor work, but I didn't know silk was so hard to work at. I'm awfully anxious to have you come.

That song is beautiful. I played it this noon when Bennie and Mama were sitting at the table; Ma looked up and Pa's eyes filled with tears. He said, "The words to that song must be awfully sad. My, that air makes me lonesome." I used to cry every time I played it, but I've gotten pretty well used to it, now.

Laurence, I disobeyed you. I risked going across the river yesterday. We were liable to go through anytime or any place. Pa walked near me, so he could pull me out if I fell in. He had to carry me part of the way 'cause there was so much water on the ice. Dan asked me for the dance tonight, couldn't go on account of river. Darn. I had two "invites," Carl and Leon, for the last dance; that was the night of the play.

Why, I don't know whether I'm glad or sorry that you are twenty. I wish you were always twenty and I always eighteen. Oh, dear, I don't want to get old. I'm not enjoying these pleasant days 'cause I know there must be some worse days in store for me.

When I get to be quite old, an old lady, I think I'll live in Elk River. The old ladies in Elk River have a party every week. Worse than the young people! Big times.

I just got through reading **Mill on the Floss**. I liked it awfully well. Leslie made a fuss, and said the only difference between it and a dime novel was that it didn't cost a dime. I told Miss Van that Leslie made an awful lot of fun of me 'cause I was reading a dime novel. She said for me to tell him it was one of the classic novels, and she liked it immensely. I came back and told Mr. Bailey. He didn't know what to do. The boys laughed at him plenty. Ever read it? Fine.

I liked Maggie and I was so sorry she had so much trouble. Lucy is so sweet, I wish she actually lived. Philip reminds me of Ruth Atkins in some ways, so of course I liked him. I almost fell in love with Stephen. Tom was too harsh. If I'd been Maggie, I'd quit loving him long ago. Best book I ever read except **Little Women**.

Glad your pa is better.

Goodbye

March 26, 1904

Oh, Laurence,

Willie Conway was eight and I was six. We thought lots of each other and he gave me some of his cards. He used to hitch his big Newfoundland to his sled or wagon and ride me to school in Otsego. We ate our dinners together regardless of the others around us and shared our apples, cakes, etc. He lived where Mr. Robbins lives now, on the big hill.

I used to go up there and swing, too. I went up to stay overnight, sometimes, with his older sister, but she was twelve, too old for me, almost.

Then we'd go in the barn and have regular plays, curtains and a hay mound for a stage. Horse blankets served as curtains. We had seats fixed for an audience, too. One part was a man who had gone to war, and, oh, he was so sorry to leave his wife at home. He was away for years and years, but finally returned. I imagined the rest. She flew into his arms and both were so weak, first one would fall and the other would hold him up and they kept bobbing up and down that way. I never took that part. Nellie always did.

Oh, dear! I remember how he used to kiss me. Oh, I'd get so mad. Cry, too. But he could never resist the temptations. Once when we came home from school there was a crowd of older pupils with us and I told him he wouldn't go to Heaven if he didn't quit kissing me. He was tickled when he thought it over and wanted to know the way to the other place immediately. Oh, I was mad.

They only stayed here a year, then went to Minneapolis to live and I didn't see them again. One day last summer (no, two years ago), I was in the woods with Joe and Bennie looking for butternuts. I came to three young men with guns on their shoulders. One of them I knew, and didn't pay any attention to the other. Robbie told him who I was; he came up to me and said very politely, "Here's some more people that don't know me; I'm Willie Conway."

"Willie Conway? How do you do!"

We shook hands and talked. He had grown so large. He was eighteen now. I guess he thought I had grown too, 'cause I was so very small until I was twelve. And then I suddenly began to shoot up. I was so tall and slim at sixteen. Hadn't seen each other for ten years. I haven't seen him since that time in the woods, but I hear he's married now.

Now I told you, though not in story form. Yours was written up nicely, too.

Good night.

March 27, 1904

Dear Laurence,

It was reported that you stood on the river bank about an hour and looked across the river as far as you could see, but didn't dare cross. I intended to go over that day, but it was so windy. I went the next day, Saturday. I might have seen you accidentally if I had gone Friday. The fates seem to be contra us anyway. Lord!

B.B.D.

March 29, 1904

I can't tell you how I feel. I want to see you as badly as you do me. Awfully pretty out tonight. Light as day and the moon is smiling down on the silvery ponds. I've skated until I can skate no more. I wished you could have been here.

Laurence, the best place to learn to dance is in bed. Try it. I learned a new dance after I went to bed last night. That's where I get most of my inspirations.

Anna

Dancing in bed.

April 19, 1904

Dear Laurence,

That was a pleasant surprise to have you come up when I didn't expect you, especially when there was a dance and I had no other invitation. I had a fine time except when Lucile acted crazy. You can dance alright; why didn't you dance more? Did you get along alright when you danced with Lucile? When you swing, face the lady you are dancing with, let her put her right hand on your shoulder and put your hand on top of hers.

Your pictures are fine. Thank you so much. I'm going to have some good ones when I graduate. Blanche Atkins is going to give me one of her pictures. So is Joe Libby.

Mama wants to know where you're working so she can go and see you. She is never going to let me go to Minneapolis again; she was too lonesome when I was gone. So lonesome that she came upstairs after something and she sat down and cried when she saw my picture.

Dorothy came in to see Bennie today. He thinks "she's a wonder, a treasure, a prize."

If we can find a good man to work for us next summer, Ma and Pa are going home to New England and to New Brunswick to spend the summer and I'll keep house. Won't that be fun?

Laurence, you'll have to return that handkerchief and mind, don't let anyone see it. Even Mama doesn't want anyone to know that her daughter could do that kind of work. I made it when I was practicing for the school entertainment and the senior play and taking five studies. I did it in the night when I was half asleep. You'd better let me try it again.

You forgot your music again. I'm glad you can sing it again when you come. I guess this yellow pencil of yours is going to last forever. I've used it since last fall.

Anna

P.S. Laurence I've had a happy thought! I'm going to give Leslie a little book on manners for his birthday. When is it?

Ma guessed that your father was 58. Pa guessed that he was 50 or 52. He must have worked awfully hard or been sickly all his life to look as old as that at 45. I think Papa looks awfully old at 49.

I think I'll have to get Susan to comb my hair for me, so I'll know how people like it. I wish I could see myself as others see me so I'd know just what to do to be attractive. I think I'll try doing my hair up farther back. Glad you told me. Tell Susan I can send her a curl if she wants to play with my hair very badly. I think I'll take a look at hers next time. I'll bet it doesn't look any better than mine does. Conceit?

April 27,1904

Dear Laurence,

I've been reading Romona for the last two days. You ought to read it, or have you? Most interesting book I ever read. Awfully heavy though. I thought Mill on the Floss was heavy, but there was a light scene once in a while. I'll bet even you would cry when Allesandro, Romona's husband, is shot. I admit that I did, and plenty. I don't expect I can read another book for a long while—two months.

Why, Laurence, I understood you to say that your Pa was 45 when you were here. Perhaps you said nearly 54, but I remember I was going out of the room just then and I didn't catch it straight. He looks lots younger than Pa. I'm going to have white hair some day; I want to so badly. Silvery.

Arthur Dare was born in 1850.

My, you people have parties often. It would be fine if you got a rig, but you don't want to spend your hard earned money that way. I should be contented with a walk, or get your uncle Robert Dare's horse. We're such a good customer, that he might let you take his horse, to come and see a customer. Mama thinks he's the closest man she ever knew. He didn't even knock off a quarter on ma's bedroom set. They all do where you buy lots. You needn't tell him. Guess she will.

I couldn't sing for a farm. Impossible. I used to when I was little. The boarders at Uncle Frank's used to give me pennies when I sang or spoke. I saved over seven dollars in pennies that way. I put it in my wheel, the first wheel I had. Also, the $5 gold piece Grandma gave me when "I was an orphan" (when Mama was at the hospital). Pa gave me the rest except $13 I made by raffling my violin. That Fournier grit is all spent now. I ask for things and get them all so easily that I don't waste my energy in earning them. That wheel was nice. Absolutely mine. I earned it.

Ma told Pa that I put your picture in my room so that it could look at my picture all the time. I didn't think of that when I put it there. I'm going to have some expensive pictures taken when I graduate. Can't afford it now.

The evening after the dance Ma got into bed with me and I didn't notice it. When I got up I was so surprised when she told me she had slept with me 'cause I'm always the first one to wake up in the night if there is a noise in the barn or the cattle get out, etc. I never was so tired as I was after that dance. She said that when she got into bed, I said, "My, you take up lots of room." It's awful to talk in your sleep. One time Mr. Hildreth told his wife what he was going to get her for Christmas, in his sleep.

Love,
Freckles

May 17, 1904

Dear Laurence,

I was so surprised to get your letter Thursday evening. I was glad, too, because I was lonesome, being all sole alone. Joe and Bennie were at Mr. Robbins's and Pa and Ma at Anoka. When Bessie comes, I'm going to take her to church at St. Michael. Take a pretty lunch and eat it in the woods. Picnic.

I got the prettiest flowers and the rooms look so pretty. I wish you were coming tomorrow. A big bunch of blue and one of yellow violets, plum blossoms, straw lilies and "Dutchman's breeches." I'll try and have wild roses when you come. I love roses.

I had the worst dream. I thought I went up in Bessie's room and she was lying motionless. When I came nearer I found to my horror that she was dead—had been murdered. I couldn't do a thing for a long time but just gaze at her. Then, I put my hand over her heart and it was still; I kissed her and started to go downstairs and I saw a hatchet covered with blood and it looked as though it had gone three inches deep into her body, but I didn't see any wound. Awful!

Dan and I had a splendid walk to the lamppost and a fine run back. We went out in the rain to make our hair curl.

That gum was just fine. Please send me some more. Mama stole mine. That orange flavor tasted so good. Danke.

I don't see what fun there is in fishing. I remember seeing you and Leon start off once last spring. Don't go to sleep and let the fish drag you into the river.

Mat met Mama the other day and politely lifted his hat. I don't believe he ever did it before in his life. He wanted to show her he knew a little something too.

Last week Walter Kirk gave Sophia such a pretty description of Anna wearing a white dress and standing by a bonfire near the road when he went by that Sophia said she would envy me if I wasn't her third cousin.

My deportment in school is something awful. Friday I ran up against Leslie and nearly knocked him over. At noon I ran into William S. and just escaped his open arms.

I'm going to teach you how to dance when you come, if you want to.

Defessa *is Latin for "tired."*

Goodbye,
Defessa

There was always swimming at the river for those who didn't like to fish.

May 28, 1904

Dear Laurence,

Of course, you can come to see me Sunday afternoon. Come early.

Those plans are excellent. We'll have a picnic. You can take me as far as the ferry Saturday evening. I may not go but I want to go everywhere before June 1. I'll tell you of my bold plans for the month of June. I won't feel like going Saturday evening after I have worked all day Saturday. I don't know of any place you could meet me except at the church.

Defessus means "tired." *Defessa Puella*. Latin.

You ought not to make me waste two cents just to tell me you could come, when you knew I wanted you to. I hope you'll get this before Saturday.

Two cents was the cost of a postage stamp to mail a letter.

Sincerely yours indeed,
Deacon Fournier

June 16, 1904

My dear,

It will be simply faire if you can come Sunday. Only
don't come in the evening. I've never been to Big Lake.
I hope it will be a nice day. Please come if you possibly can. I'd be so disappointed if you didn't.

Saturday evening I heard some noise in the sitting
room. I opened the door and stood face to face with a
most hideous looking man. I started to look at a book
he handed me, and I felt that he was moving towards
me so I moved swiftly to the back kitchen door and he
followed me, but sat there near the door. All he could
say was, "Please God, overnight, one night."

He couldn't or wouldn't understand that I didn't want
him. I sent him to the barn. Soon he came back, and
smiling triumphantly said, "No man there."

I ran to the barn and he after me, but I found Uncle
Fred there, and delivered the man over to him. I was
going to run to a neighbor next, if Uncle hadn't been
in the barn. I didn't know what I was doing until I
thought it over later. Since then I've been so nervous
that I start at every sound. My, I was scared!

The strawberries will be just fine if you come Sunday. Saturday afternoon at three, you can make a mental picture of me making a strawberry shortcake. I never
made one.

"Fare thee well, and if forever, still forever, Fare thee
well."

*The Fournier
land was acces-
sible to tramps,
hobos, stray
animals, travel-
ers, and even
thieves crossing
the river or
coming from
Dayton,
Monticello or
Rogers.*

*Anna's writing
shows that
strangers often
asked for food, to
spend the night,
or to feed their
horses.*

July 5, 1904

Laurie dear,

It does sound romantic, the way you tell of your difficulties in coming over to see me. A year ago today was the day we took that long cycle ride. Tell "Little Watch" not to get lonesome, Little Girl will play with her next Sunday. I know my dear, it must be hard for you to save your money if you inherited that "wanting to spend" from both parents. I do try so hard to sympathize but I have always been taught to pinch and save since I can remember.

I hope Joe and Bennie won't be extravagant. They aren't now. They didn't want to go to Elk River the Fourth because they'd have to pay ten cents ferrage. Did you suppose I meant that I didn't care if you saved your gold or not? When you spoke of it that day it made me mad for a minute and I thought, Why should I care?

Thinking it over later, I decided that if I didn't care for your money I didn't care for you because the ability to keep your money is what is going to make you. I am very anxious that you will succeed and I'm sure you're going to be a smart man. It would be too bad if you weren't, because you have a good start and your Mama and Father think so much of you, and your Mama has brought you up so nicely and everyone in Elk River and Otsego speaks so highly of you. For my sake, try. There aren't many young men of your age that are getting the wages that you are getting.

Yes, Sweethearts for a year over, and never quarreled. That's rare. If I have anything to say about it, I am sure we will still be keeping so on my twentieth birthday. Yes, I hope so—with all my heart.

I just got that present from you. I was so surprised 'cause I didn't expect anything. It cheered me up beau-

Little Watch: see cover portrait. A gift from Laurence. They took turns keeping it. Anna's initials, ADF, were on the back. The face is blue; the numbers are red.

tifully. I was just feeling very badly over something that I will tell you about Sunday.

The letter sealing wax set is just what I've been wanting ever since I heard of them. It isn't worth money to me—money wouldn't get it away because you gave it to me. You'll have to show me how to use that wax. I can never thank you enough for it.

I got lots of presents from my one thousand cousins in New Brunswick. A prayer book, a woolen blanket that my cousin spun and wove by hand, little baskets and boxes and pincushions.

Seven years ago today my brother Frankie died. I am writing something in a little book every day, like your little book. The family gave me a lovely toilet case for my birthday.

Au revoir,
Hannah Phournyer

July 17, 1904

Dear Laurence,

Joe and Ben think the world of the baseball mitt you gave them. They won't have any trouble over it 'cause they have planned to catch ten balls with it and if they catch all, that boy has it for ten more balls. Bennie thought it was funny when you said, "How do you know Laurence will give him a cookie," and I said, because I wanted you to.

If you tell me that you can come Sunday after my birthday, I'll keep you some birthday cake. I have my work all planned for next year. I'll practice piano one-half hour after I get home from school. Then one hour with Joe (probably accompanying his singing). Study from seven 'til twelve. Then sew one hour. Read Sunday night and sleep Saturday night when I don't go to a party or dance that night.

Anna's birthday was July 14, 1885.

Read German and French fifteen minutes apiece each day. And I think that will be about all I can stand besides doing my room work and going so far to and from school.

We're having a pretty bad time now. Uncle Fred broke his back, Joe ran a huge nail in his foot, and Bennie ran one of those handles on the cultivator half way through his side. I guess he was hurt quite badly, so I had a pretty hard time looking after the three.

I simply can't think of anything more to write, but I want a nice long letter Monday.

Au revoir, cher,
Bridge N. Cook

July 20, 1904

I'm awfully anxious to have you come or at least hear from you. You must come Sunday.

I'm lonesome to play with Little Watch and talk with Laurie dear. I haven't gone to a single thing since the banquet and I'm about wild from being lonesome. I'll teach you how to dance this time even if it is Sunday. I wished I could have been at the bowery dance the Fourth. I haven't danced a step since the last dance you took me to, that very exciting time.

Bowery dances were in or close to Dayton; sometimes a little wild.

I look at that seal and wax all the time, anxious to try it. I've come back now; while I was writing I heard Mr. Gray's voice call, "Annie." I went down and he says, "The girls said that Editor would be coming around pretty soon and you'd want some flowers." He had a huge bouquet, so now you must come. There's a beautiful rose, I wish I could send it to you.

That's all for today. I've got to comb my hair. Ma said she saw lots of pretty girls, but none with hair like mine. Sound nice? I'll write more tomorrow.

March 13 was the anniversary of the night they met at Blanche's "Poverty Party."

March 13 was a dear night for us, wasn't it.

Goodbye, *Chere*

July 23, 1904

My dear,

I spent the afternoon with Kitten and bid farewell to Ruth who is going to the St. Louis Exposition. We acted like fools as usual. We ate ice cream soda, of which I swallowed the most, one dozen plums, four peaches and an immense supper.

Betty Kitten: a classmate.

Ice cream was still new to smaller towns.

You were awfully pleasant last Sunday. You are always to me, but this was in the superlative. We ought to try to be happy when we are together; we seldom enjoy that privilege.

Of course I am awfully proud of you, too. I don't suppose that counts very much towards giving you encouragement, but I am. So nice of you to keep your geld. Thank you for all the pretty appellations. Yes, indeed, "She wants to be wanted," dear. We certainly shall be keeping company next year if you agree.

You must come up oftener, though. I should never have ceased to grieve if we had never found Little Watch. Then you'd had to kiss me, but you probably wouldn't have thought of it and I'd have been safe. Yes, perhaps some day you may, without my hurting Petite Montre.

Petite Montre: French for "Little watch."

That was a splendid walk to the river. Very exciting when a cloud came up. I enjoyed it when I saw the danger was past. A ring is too conspicuous. Aren't we happy?

I'll show you my petit livre next time. Not very interesting.

The splendid walk—probably when Laurence gave Anna the ring they called "ghost ring"— most likely a Bloodstone ring.

Susan and another girl were coming from the depot when Kitten and I were by the courthouse. One of them waved; Betty caught my arm and made me wave. I dare not think what they thought of me. The school children here think you're cute looking (according to Bessie). They must have gotten that from their elders.

One day Mr. Gray was teasing me and I said, "Please quit; editor's alright."

He says, "Of course, he's alright; he's a fine fellow." I asked him how he had found that out, and he says, "Oh, well, I hear a good deal about all those boys in town."

Little Watch wasn't lost at all. It was on the piano in an envelope with a commencement invitation. I leaped for joy when I found it. I was so happy to think that you trust me with anything which I consider so precious. I shall never dare ask you to trust me again, but one good consolation for me is that you said you cared more for Little Girl than for Little Treasure. You can protect Little Treasure now. It'll be safer.

"Little Treasure" is the cherished watch.

Lucile told me how she and Clara had registered as Mr. and Mrs. Kerwott and Mr. and Mrs. Walters at a swell hotel in Buffalo. Awful!!!

Next Wednesday I shall expect a letter from Laurie addressed to Me, Anna Delia Fournier, Dayton, Minn. I'm going to visit grandma most of the time, also Sophia, and Olive and Miss Morris. I'll probably get lonesome, so I should like a nice long, fat letter, if you please on Wednesday.

Au revoir

August 3, 1904

Laurie, my dear,

John Hamlett said, "Anna goes with a young man from St. Paul."

John Hamlett was a neighbor in Otsego.

Bennie said, "Yes."

John says, "How many dozen other girls has he that Anna doesn't know of?"

Bennie was mad and he said very emphatically: "Not any others!! Just Anna!" Hamlett didn't believe it.

A great many people have asked me, "Do you suppose that a young man like him will stay at home evenings and Sundays and be lonesome? Those city boys go with dozens of girls." I don't say much. What can I do, except fight against hideous thoughts, pray and trust you. So you see that you're not the only one who suffers. They don't know you as I do or they wouldn't say that.

Mama will never let me go camping. French people don't believe in it. I'd be the talk of the state if I went.

We had two nice head of cattle killed by lightning Friday night. Some men are here today and we'll get some money from the insurance company.

Lightning caused frequent and devastating disasters all over the country up to and during the early 1900s. Frequent reports in local newspapers recorded losses of barns, homes, cattle, and human injuries and deaths.

Goodbye, dearie.

August 12, 1904

Laurie,

I was very much surprised to get that last epistle. I looked for you last Sunday but didn't think you'd come because I knew that you were all in St. Paul and wouldn't be likely to come up for one day.

I intended to send Joe and Bennie after Mr. Gray's boat. Meanwhile we would walk to the river. Then we would have our ride while the boys were in swimming. Then, when we were tired of rowing, we could have a lunch on the bank. How would that be? We can do it another time.

Visit to an old, dying friend.

Mr. Guyer, one of our friends, is dying. I went to see him yesterday, and I can't get him out of my mind. He is so weak that he can't speak above a whisper. He didn't know me until Al told him it was "Anna, Adele's girl." He was awfully glad to see me because few people go now; they went six weeks ago.

He held my hand a long time and I was almost scared of him. There isn't anything left of him. We can see every bone in his hands. His eyes are glassy. He'd whisper things to his son that he wanted to say to me. Oh, I felt so bad for the old man.

"We're going to have a telephone."

Yes, dear, we're going to have a telephone. I have one now. Rather diminutive though. Shall I expect you on August 7?

Goodnight. So dark I can't see.

August 13, 1904

Laurie, my dear:

It is 8:45 and the men have just got thru' their supper. How would you like to be a farmer? I've had a great deal of exercise today. I ironed, did housework more than usual, which is a lot, played piano, washed windows, jumped over branches (for practice), ran nearly a quarter of a mile without stopping, went after the big canvas a circus nearby 'way out by Orton's, and now I'm writing. Isn't that quite a lot for me to do in one day? Pa is awfully glad he cut grain last Sunday because he was put back two days by rain.

Oh, you ought to see me in my new wrapper. Do you know what it is? Well, it's a very loose dress. It's red, and plain and has four big gold buttons down the front. It's long and drags. I like it because no one knows whether I am Mrs. Paul or the little mosquito that I am. I really wish I was bigger, but not taller.

It won't be long before we can be together again. I am so pleased that you were happy last Sunday. And I made you happy! You don't want to get over it until you come again.

I think I ought to read that story about the "ghost ring." Don't call it that, it scares me. Find some other cute as well as appropriate name for it. I always think of a ghost as being wicked and the ring we have is sacred, and the apparition is holy, isn't it? Yes, dear, it is there - it is truly. Most certainly, happiness is in chains.

"It is to have and to hold."

Dearest, I won't send back our Little Watch unless you demand it. I'm going to keep that from Mama and it's all our own. Yes, I'll furnish the cake. I'll make it myself. Two dozen bananas ought to be a great sufficiency. I wish we could bring ice cream. They wouldn't be as likely to have that as fruit.

A year earlier, on July 13, 1903, Anna responded to LAD's letter by turning down a buggy ride to Monticello unless another couple and a chaperone were present.

My, the weeks fly. Three more before school commences. The time seems long but when we think back, it's short. Glory! A year ago I didn't begin to care for you until July 13, and never thought of the thing you refer to until we broke the wishbone.

Once when Ma was away, I, unobserved, could see Bennie smile by himself. I asked him why. After fifteen minutes' coaxing and teasing he said, "Joe says you and Laurence are 'promised.' You aren't, are you?"

"Of course not."

"You're just going with Laurence to have a feller, aren't you?"

I assured him that was true and asked him if he would be sorry if we were, and why he would be.

"Because I want you to stay here," he said.

I explained to him that wouldn't take me away and told him people had diamond rings when they were promised. He was very much grieved when I told him I had only one more year to stay with him.

Anna

August 26, 1904

Dear Laurie,

I dread awfully to have Aunt Ovila visit us. She has a mansion of a house and Lillie, her daughter, can play on a piano. We expected her today. Probably she'll come tomorrow. I guess she likes me pretty well though, 'cause I go with American people a great deal.

Lillie is to be married to an American so she would naturally like them. She dislikes French ways. I've decided to forget the French language entirely 'cause when I talk English I have to stop and think of what I'm going to say, and I can't help but use French idioms. I have to struggle against them constantly.

I've been awfully lonesome today. This afternoon I dreamt we had built a straw shed larger than the barn and you and I were out to look at it. It looked like the barn as it was when Bennie was a new baby. The French way of saying, "How much," is to say, "How big do you like me?" Whenever we asked that of Ben, he always liked us "as big as a barn." One time Joe asked him that, and he happened to hate him. Half an hour later Joe asked him again and he thought there was no need of Joe's asking him again, so he says, "When I hate, I hate all the time." No one around had a barn like ours and it was the biggest thing Bennie had ever seen. I found this among his valentines:

> "Pretty Dorothy," Bennie said,
> and there caused a dash of red
> through the brow across his cheek.
> "Boys are strong and girls are weak,
> so I'll carry, if you will,
> Dorothy's basket up the hill."

Did our trip cost you an awful lot? Must have. Yes, you've been patient and have been a gentleman and I give you credit for it, but "sometime" is the only reward I can afford now. I did intend to let you kiss me one little once, but since your last letter, I decided differently. It scares me.

Goodbye.
A.D.F.

August 29, 1904

Laurie, my dear,

I had a lovely time camping yesterday, but I don't think I'd care to stay up there all week. Not with all those hungry boys to cook for. Those pipes! I wonder if Dud and Fred and William don't think they are "pre-possessing in their appearances"?

I enjoyed the ride immensely, too. Wasn't the moon beautiful? And you were good, too. That made me so happy. Do it always, please? Did you hear Lucile "boss" the girls up there? I can't live where someone is continually pawing and scrapping. I'm a peaceable party. I went to sleep quick last night. After being so cold (you didn't know how cold I was), when I did get warm I went to sleep quick. I took the lamp chimney to bed with me.

I've told Mama nearly everything already. Glory, that day used me all up. I can hardly wiggle today. My right arm is frightfully swollen up and every time I move it I howl. That's from having played ball.

Goodbye.

September 3, 1904

Well, Aunt Ovila came today. Not as bad as I expected. She talks all the time. She's awfully quick. Neat. Can't you come next Sunday, dear? I'll have to stay all alone with the boys the whole day. I'll be awfully lonesome and you say that if you don't come this Sunday, you can't for a long time. Let's not go to the dance, though. Please come, dearie.

Anna's budget plan for Laurence.

After Sunday, you must begin to save your money. You must tell me you have put $5 in the bank every week, never to be taken out. I calculate it this way; you pay $3 for board, and two dollars a week spending money ought to do. Then you could save $5 every week easy.

In ten weeks you would have $50. Think of it! Then you would have two months in which to earn Christmas money. If you do that, you will be the nicest boy ever. If you don't, you will be nice anyway, but.

I went for a long ride tonight, but it was so hot that I don't feel much better for it. The moon looks just the same as it did last Sunday evening. You looked awfully nice up there.

Well, Ma says it's going to storm so I had better retire so I can get some rest before I get killed. Eddie the hired man, says if the house was burning and I fainted, he'd carry me out, so I feel perfectly safe. Isn't he good? If you were here, though, I wouldn't let him do it, of course.

Goodbye.

September 4, 1904

Laurie my dear,

I didn't intend to write tonight, but I've been scared into wakefulness so I can do nothing else. It made me so nervous that it's impossible to go to sleep. About half an hour ago (nine o'clock), Joe went out of doors and saw a man looking in Mama's bedroom window.

Our hired man happened to be out at the same time. Joe was so sure it was Eddie that he says, "Eddie, what are you doing there," and laughed at him.

The man didn't answer and slipped around the corner of the house, after stumbling over the cellar trap door, a block, and a few other things. Then, Joe ran to the barn and Eddie was there whistling and calmly bedding the horses.

Joe came in and told us, but he didn't say much about it because he was afraid he had been mistaken. Later, Eddie came in and informed us that there was a man here who wanted to stay overnight. It was storming so that Papa hated to send him off at that time of night. He wouldn't come in the house, we never let anyone sleep in the barn, so he started for town. He looked as though he'd been drinking. The idea of his looking in through the window that way! I'm afraid he'll come back and sleep in the barn, and then go off and take a horse with him, or set fire in the hay. Dear! Vassar won't take him across the river by ferry as late as this, and in this storm, with the logs running as thick as they are, he isn't a very smart tramp.

I'm going to take English, Literature, English History, Chemistry, Commercial Arithmetic and Civics or Commercial Law. I told Mr. Dunkeline that I was going to be good the first half, and the last half of the year I'd let loose all that pent up badness. I'm going to work this first half. I dread to go tomorrow 'cause it's so muddy. I'll have to wear my short skirt, I guess.

Skirts were still floor length, or ankle length at least. A short skirt would have fallen closer to the floor than the knees.

Did you have a good time yesterday, dear? I did, considering the length of time we were together. I'd gone to the train, only I knew you'd rather I wouldn't, so I didn't. I knew you the minute I caught sight of you a block away. When you write again to Leslie, you'll let me put in a little note for him, won't you?

Papa said that he had heard worms bore their way into nuts, so there! You needn't think that's a lie. I'll never tell you another thing, however. Perhaps that seems as impossible to you as living after having had an operation in one's head did to some people who didn't know much. Now, you don't know much about worms or insects.

That was a terrible mistake I made yesterday, dearest, to tell you I didn't expect you over as early as that. Pardon me, please, won't you? I'm a thoughtless wretch. I always want you to come as early as you possibly can and go as late as you can. I never thought how that sounded until Ma told me.

I guess I'll retire. I don't care if that man comes and kills me.

Farewell

September 14, 1904

Glory! I wheeled to Dayton and back home. I visited grandma all day. My, she told me lots about her childhood and girlhood. She gave me an awfully funny nut that came from China. Last Sunday she had sent me a lovely box of bon bons.

I saw an old man that was 86 years old and he had a better memory than I have, I believe. He told about when he learned to smoke when he was a little fellow. Funny!

The new church at Dayton will be wonderful. It will be dedicated at Christmas. You ought to come.

Goodbye.
Anna

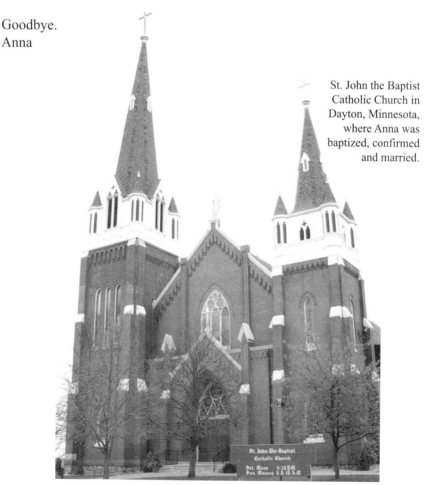

St. John the Baptist Catholic Church in Dayton, Minnesota, where Anna was baptized, confirmed and married.

September 18, 1904

Laurie, Oh, dear.

I'm so anxious to have you come again. It's so lone-some!!

I got a new picture today. Cecilia's. Awfully good.

My dear! I'm so proud of you! I'm so happy to think you are saving your money. Why, that's a whole lot of money in the bank. You're almost rich. I didn't sup-pose you had any money at all. Yes, indeed, dearest, I'm so very light hearted that I almost float in air. Glory. I don't know what to do. I'll never be able to teach. I can't afford to go to college, don't want to go to Nor-mal School and ashamed to stay at home. No career for me except to lie down and die. I wouldn't be strong enough to be a hired girl, so I think I'll give myself to the Pa of Waters.

Oh, I've thought of a name for the picture in the door: "Bashful Little Sweethearts," or, "If you kiss me, I'll ."

Goodbye.
Anna

September 20, 1904

My dear,

You'll think it's funny to get a letter so soon, but I want to tell you some things. This week is the street fair at Anoka. George and Lucile are going to be together Friday, Saturday and Sunday. I can't get Silly to go mit mir. I can't go and meet you, especially on Saturday.

I also received an invitation from Anna Murphy to spend street fair time with her.

And now listen, do you hear? Do you realize? Ain't I good? If you will show yourself when you get to Anoka, I will come home on the train with you and get off at Elk River at four o'clock. Wouldn't that be better than just seeing you a minute at Elk River? Don't let anyone else sit with you. All the other kids are coming home on the late train, but I can't come home in the night; so it's an excellent excuse.

Laurence, tell me truly, you aren't going to work up there at Duluth. If you do, I won't let you go. I have heard too much about boys getting spoiled in that wicked city. Besides, you'd spend all your money up there with Leslie and I wouldn't see you for years.

Duluth: that wicked city.

Oh, dear, I'm so sorry you are sick. My, you must hurry up and get well or your Mama won't let you go to Duluth. Be awful good to yourself so you won't get pneumonia. Don't get discouraged, dear, you're doing famously. After you get $100 in the bank, it will come in lots faster and you won't notice it. But it seems an age before you can get $100.

See if you can't get that amount before Christmas. I should feel very badly if you spent your money foolishly when I don't want you to spend money in entertaining me and try so hard to help you save it.

We can never have that neat little cottage if you don't help me. Poor Petite Montre, indeed. You made a mis-

take. It's $1800, because if we have a house we have
no piano to buy. There's one thing I forgot before. It's
a big piano lamp that stands up, with a red globe.

You'll write to me while you're up there, won't you?
Write as soon as you get this or on the way 'cause I'll
be awfully anxious about you. I hope I can see you
Saturday.

Come out on the steps of the train, at Anoka, so I'll
know where to find you. Be sure. I know you'll manage it O.K. You always do.

Goodbye dear,
A.D.F.

September 29, 1904

You needn't be mad at Vassar. He told the school kids they'd better be nice to me 'cause I was pretty swell. "She goes with that printing man's son, you know."

Oh, yes, they all know now. "He's alright."

Up camping, Bess Opitz said the Jamiesons (the last people I'd think of) said something awfully nice about me. "Years ago there was a nice little girl lived in Elk River. Looking at Anna Delia Fournier, they saw this nice girl." Speaking of Anna led them to talk about Laurence Dare and Leslie. From the way she spoke, I judged it was something pretty nice. Of course, they're related to Les.

Classmates.

Miss Churchill didn't attempt to pronounce my name. Miss Marchand is the only one that did. Miss Churchill is cute when she laughs. She's little and round shouldered and awfully big around the waist.

Guess what I saw this morning? Swaggie sitting with Bessie on the steps at the Star News office, talking very earnestly. Coila must have had her principles in her boots when she went with him and allowed him to spend money on her.

Coila Dare: cousin of Laurence who had reputation as a flirt.

I'm afraid you're working hard. Your face looked thinner than usual, I thought. Take good care of yourself. My dear, we are young only once, you know. I don't practice what I preach, but do as I tell you and not as I do. Please write me a nice long letter Friday.

"'Tis a beautiful day to be glad in."

Au revoir.
A.D.F.

October 1, 1904

Mr. Laurence Albee Dare,

I got my picture taken last Saturday. Perhaps I can exchange with Leslie? If I were you I would not trust Leslie with all that stuff that you told him.

Sunday, we got up too late to go to church so we went to the river and in the woods. At night, after we had retired, Papa began to play on the violin, and Bessie thought she had never heard such a wonderful violin, so I had to play piano with Pa. Then, Papa played waltzes and other dances, and we danced to our hearts' content. I know a new dance, too. Delightful!

We have eight men working for us this week. Isn't that a large family? Makes me think of the nobility. So many servants. We are going to have the threshers by next Saturday. Oh, Dear! Five meals!

A week from next Saturday I have been invited to spend the day with Lucile Hildreth. Little Falls is going to play with Elk River that day. St. Cloud beat Elk River 43 to 0 in football last Saturday. We girls hope to do better than that in basketball. The High School team includes Silly, Betty, Nellie, Eaton, Mabel, Etta and me. Mixed team is Blanche R., Lilian Daskan, Alice Beck, Cecil, Lucile Hindley, and Ruth Atkins.

How can you expect ever to get rich if you spend your gold like that. You mustn't become spoiled. When I earn money, I'm going to wear white lawn dresses and be poor and save my money, and buy a claim like Miss Brown, and live on it and take care of chickens.

Anna D. Fournier

November 3, 1904

Dear Laurie,

"November skies are gray."

This morning just after Ma arose, she looked out to the barn and saw Pa shakin' hands with a stranger. Then she recognized her oldest brother Brazell who lives near Pembina, North Dakota. He hadn't come for four years, since Grandpa's golden wedding. He said Ma knew how to kiss but I did it better. Good?

Mama is his baby sister and he likes her. I believe he must be an ideal husband (but Papa is more ideal, of course). He has always been awfully unlucky. He's the one that lost his barn to fire last year, you know. This summer his entire crop, 900 acres of wheat, was destroyed by hail. His wife and grown up daughter have been awfully sick and there's always something wrong with them.

Laurie dear, what would my dear like for Christmas? Lucile wants a silver toilet set with "Lucile" engraved on the back about this deep. Extravagant. She'll get it, too.

Don't ask me what I want. I have everything I want, except several things I can't have, so of course I don't want them.

Your Ma's canary will cost so much that you'll have to take the money that you were to put on my present. I've had my turn anyway. You've spent tons for rigs, music, etc.

Little Watch wants me to retire.

Farewell.

P.S. My, we're having some beautiful days. Nettie and I went down to the Elk River where you used to live on Main Street. OH! It's pretty! It was such a clear day. I wished I had your field glass.

Mr. Norval took me up on top of the school house last week. I'd never been there before.

Lucile's piece is about boys. When she was rehearsing, she had to say, "Boys are disagreeable things." Miss Keatley said she didn't say it as though she believed it at all. Pretty good of her.

Let me tell you something funny. The German II class is reading Imensee. Art Bailey couldn't translate this: "He lifted her in his arms and carried her through the under brush."

Miss D. got mad and she says, "Well, Arthur, can't you translate that? What would he naturally do if she couldn't get through? Perhaps your experiences are limited, but you may have to do it someday." (That reminded me of when Reinhard and Elizabeth were out botanizing. Do you remember?)

The boys have gone fishing again tonight. When Ray went last Sunday night, he caught a fifteen pound one. Mr. Gray said it was huge.

Oh, Nettie says there's a place in my eyes that you can see right through. I told her it was just my "bery brilliant brains."

That's as bad as Shirley Mills seeing way down into Alice's eyes.

Goodbye dear,
Anna

November 11, 1904

My dear Laurence,

I feel better. I was so glad to get your letter, dear. I didn't expect one now 'til Friday; it was so good. Willie always calls me when there is a letter from you, so I get it right away. I feel quite happy these days. It seemed an age since you came through.

You were very brave not to get scared of those wolves or the dark ever. You must think an awful lot of me to stand all that just to come to see an insignificant little rustic French maid.

Wolves in the woods of Otsego.

We mustn't think of being married for a long time. I'll teach next year; it will take me four years in college, then I'll teach four years. I'll have to do some sewing for a year and then I'll be ready. That won't be long. Olive F. and Henry have been engaged for ten, twelve or fourteen years. That's worse than us. They see each other every day, though.

Please don't say you're homely. You're too sweet for anything. Nettie Thomas thinks you're the most distinguished looking young man she ever saw. "He looks as though there was something in him that was worth something."

Seventy-five dollars! Glory! We're almost rich. $100 by January! Oh, dear! Are you going to spend $20 for Christmas? I'll be lucky if I have five dollars. I don't know what to get for you. I had gotten some little sachet powder bags last summer, but have given them away. Please tell me what you want.

I finished Jean Valjean last night. I never enjoyed reading a book so much. I think Jean is the most admirable character in fiction. I didn't find it deep or heavy, either. My, I like him. Wish I were Cosette.

*Jean Valjean was Victor Hugo's main character in **Les Miserables**.*

Oh, my dearest, I try so hard to be a good girl for Laurie, dear. I pray about a half hour a day. Our priest said that prayer is the only thing that could make men

The Little Watch.

holy and I believe it, don't you. I'm so careful mit Der Kleine Uhr. I'm so happy to think you trust me with it for so long. I was selfish to have kept it, though.

Yes, I wore it to school every day. I had trouble with it, too, but I love it all the more. I wore it in my pocket for a while, then in the folds of a full waist, but it could plainly be seen. I expected something the first day but they didn't.

Well, on Friday Carl came up to me and said, "Where did you get the watch?" I laughed and fooled with it. Two minutes later Fatty came and asked the identical thing. I did the same to him. They were nearly splitting their sides over it in the back of the room.

Then, Swaggy asked me. I looked cross and showed him that it was none of his business. At noon I asked Mabel why that was.

"They thought it funny that you wouldn't go to the train to meet him and then would wear his watch," was what I got from her. I felt quite badly. A little later Albert Hill says, "Anna's got a new watch." I paid no attention. Carl says, "Oh, see the watch! Wow, nice!" They looked at each other and laughed.

I didn't see anything laughable about it. I got mad and I shouted, "If I wear that watch, it's my business and you'd better not meddle with it, or there'll be trouble!!!! I don't think it's one bit cute or funny either!!!" Then I broke down and cried as hard as I could. My face changed from white to red to purple to black again and again. They were all perfectly astonished. I'd have talked and jawed all noon if I could have kept from crying. Just think, I had stood that teasing since March 13, 1903.

They won't tease anymore. Nettie told me they felt pretty badly over it when they saw it bothered me. Now I wear the little darling in plain sight and no one ever mentions it.

After school Nettie and I discussed some things. I don't think it's nice for girls to meet boys at places that way, especially when all the men of the town meet that train. Besides, the girls never asked me to go with them and meet you. How do you think I'd felt if I had gone and you had not come? Then, when Silly yelled, "I've got him! Come on, Bessie, he won't get away! I'm taking him straight to the hall," Bessie said she wanted to disappear through that platform. And with Mr. Stahl there. You must have heard them.

Little Watch wants me to kiss her good night and put her to bed. Guess I'll obey.

Goodbye,
Anna

November 14, 1904

My dear Laurie,

I don't think Petite Montre is lonesome for you because I pay lots more attention to her than you do. I've
found a little fob with a little heart on it that I had
when I was young. I scarred it up good and it's O.K.
It's such a dear watch. I love it! I don't think I'll wear
it to school; when I get an unlucky streak, I lose everything.

Were you afraid when you went home last night? I
woke up at two o'clock and didn't go back to sleep
until three. The wolves were howling again when I
woke up. I pitied you. When I told Ma about it, she
wanted me to take you with the horse, but you had
gone too far.

Our "private apartment," mine and Nettie's at school,
is the little room back of the laboratory that is a store
room for those big leatherbound volumes filled with
congressional reports and jiggers. Nettie and I cleaned
it good. We have a mantle, mirror, pictures, etc. Everyone compliments us on it. Mr. Stahl thinks it's O.K.
We dine there.

You didn't show me your bank book, but you said
you had $60. You're doing even better than I thought
you were.

Au revoir,
Anna

November 23, 1904

My gracious, it's lonesome these long Sunday afternoons, especially when it's so nice. I tell you we spend
some terrible, long lonesome afternoons by living on
the farm. There's no place to go. You'll be here two
weeks from today, won't you? Please, dearest. We'll
have to go and see Minnie and Henry after they get
settled. Glory, it seems funny. It's just as horrid for me
to have her marry as it would be for you if Leslie or
Laura were to go off.

Nettie and I are getting to be more inseparable ev-
eryday. I don't believe two people could be better fitted to chum together than we are. Our minds seem to
run in the same channel. It's so strange. So often she
starts to do a thing and I'm just about going to do it.
Then again I'll do something and she starts to do the
same. Or she starts to tell me something and I was just
thinking the identical. Nearly every day we do things
like that.

Thanksgiving will be here soon. Oh, say I've got an
idee. Just struck me. Can't you come that day? The
Dayton church is to be dedicated on that day. The
trouble is the anchor ice would probably be running
then. Telephone up the day before and find out if it's
nice weather.

Oh, Laurie, will you do something for me, please?
You know Nettie and I have our dining room at school
all fixed up nice. Well, last Tuesday, George K. and
Hattie M. went in and stole two awfully cute ping pong
fans, our class colors and a picture of the school house
that was nice. It was one of those blueprints mounted
on a round piece of dark brownish cardboard. I don't
want to lose it because Miss Marchand gave it to me.

If you happen to visit them sometime, will you steal
them for me? They are very precious to me. Nettie's
father gave them to her when he started for California
and she'll never see him again. Awful? And we can't

A teacher.

get any more class colors. None in town. If you'll steal those for us, we'll bless you for ever after. Please, dear. They're awful mean. They'd no right to take them than to take school property or anything else.

Come soon.
A.D.F.

November 30, 1904

My dear Laurie,

I'm awfully glad you didn't get fired. But it would have been kind of nice to have you come back. We had pretty nice times anyway. I was disappointed that I couldn't say goodbye to you, dear. I ran to the car door after you, but couldn't see you, and I looked for three minutes in vain. I looked in every window.

When the train started off, someone hollered, "There goes Laurence!" I didn't see you then. Did you see me? The next day Mr. Norval asked me if I put Laurence on the train alright.

I wish I hadn't seen those murderers. I see them all the time. I'm so nervous. I see them every time I open a door or shut my eyes. I'm so afraid to go over town.

Tonight someone knocked and I had to go to the door. Ma and I had just been talking about those men, and I shook so I could hardly stand up. I nearly had to go to bed. It's awful to be that way.

We had our class picture taken today. We had more fun. I didn't stand near Dan. Neither did I go to the dance at all. We went to the church dedication on Thanksgiving Day. They gave dinner in the old church. I wasn't feeling very good so I went to Grandpa's.

I shouldn't think it would be as well to go to a little country town because you'd spend so much for board. While if you went to Chicago, you could earn a big bonus soon. It would be awful not to see each other for so long. But I could stand it if I had to if you wrote real often and if you didn't discover that you were becoming infatuated with another and were neglecting me.

I thank God real often that we get along so well. We always did. It's so horrid to fight. Fred and Blanche had a real fight and everyone in town is talking about them. If I once got mad I'd never come back.

The "Box-car Murderers"— an infamous case in Sherburne County. This is another case of people fleeing a train at Elk River who crossed the river and passed Fournier's land.

*At that time,
bowling alleys
were mostly a
"hang out" for
men, a place of
low repute. Years
later, Laurence
did take up
bowling and won
some trophies.
He never smoked.*

Beer!!! Oh, Lord, Lord, Lord deliver my Laurie from such a (don't know of anything bad enough to call it.). I'm glad you told me of it. I'm so happy. You did not indulge! Anna is so immensely proud of you. How nice it would be if when you got to be an old man, you could say you had never tasted it.

Everyone is crazy over that bowling alley. I wouldn't be seen there. I'll bet lots of girls'll wish they hadn't been seen there after a while. Terrible. Everyone thinks Dayton is a rough town, but it's no worse than Elk River. In Elk River it's the town people that drink lots. In Dayton, it's the people from the country and from other towns. Dayton people drink in their own town; Elk River people go elsewhere to get drunk and disgrace other towns. Dayton people have a very poor opinion of Elk River. I stick up for it like sixty and I even had a fight with Olive over it once, but really it isn't what it used to be. The old people are all right. But the young folks are pretty bad.

I got my new felt shoes today. They're No. 4 and gigantic, lined throughout with long fur almost like great heavy plush. They're so warm. They all laughed at me plenty, but I guess if they had to go as far as I do, and just about died when they got their feet cold, they'd want something to keep them warm. I can't wear leather shoes in winter without freezing my heels until I can't walk.

When Papa was twenty he was ten dollars in debt when he came to Minnesota. He lived through it. We will too. I'm surely happy, so you must be also, and we'll get along alright if we trust in God. He's the one we must both look to for encouragement.

Goodbye dearest.

P.S. I expect to make my semi-annual shopping visit to Elk River next week. Ma and Pa just said the reason they get me all the things I want is I stay at home so much and don't go to two or three dances a week, etc. I don't care to go to dances except with you. It's hard on parents to have their kids out lots.

December 2, 1904

The anchor ice is running some and we may have trouble in going across tomorrow. I had an awful time getting across the river. I wish you were here to go skating.

You need not worry about Dan any more, dear. He is gone on Millie Latta and takes her to dances now. He won't have anything to do with me at all.

Write to me soon, dear, and if you don't get a letter for a long time, don't worry. I'll write as soon as I can. If I get caught on the other side of the river it won't make any difference, but if I should stay on this side, I might not get your letter for a week, and I wouldn't be able to mail one.

Oh dear, I dread that old story. I thought we'd have a bridge this fall. No one can imagine how hard it is for us on this side of the river. You start off in the morning and don't know but what you'll come back home in a hearse or else float down to Minneapolis. We have to cross where the ice is so thin that we can hear the roar of the water under us sometimes.

If I get drowned, you'll have a nice piece in the paper about me, won't you? But it isn't as dangerous in the fall as it is the spring. I'm not afraid with Papa though. He saved me once when I would have gone under the ice if he hadn't caught me that second. He knows lots about it.

Goodbye.

December 12, 1904

My dear Laurie,

Lord, Pa is playing the violin and it makes me awful lonesome. I don't want to hear music when I'm away from home. It always makes me sad. I went to a dance last night and am awfully tired. Carl took me. Oh, it was fine. I wished you could have been there. I'd have been in perfect bliss if you had.

Pa and Ma have been talking about old times when Pa first saw Ma at a dance. He played some of the tunes that they played that night. Isn't that funny.

Bess thinks you're the cutest ever. She told me she also noticed what happened up camping. I wasn't mistaken when I thought that she was gone on you, was I? Other people notice it without my calling their attention to it. She's been bragging to me how she has always gone with any boy she wanted. After a while she'll have to say, "All except Frank Chase and Laurence."

You must come at Christmas. It'll cost too much to send your little present.

Goodbye dearest.

December 15, 1904

My dear Laurie,

Of course not! Leslie and I don't love each other. But those were his words. We were dancing and were commencing to quarrel. He said, "Cousins shouldn't quarrel." I said we wouldn't. He said we'd love each other always and I agreed.

Yes, I must make a lot of good resolutions, 'cause next year I'll be alone in the world and I must be brave. I promised Mr. Stahl that I would use my influence so as to have good order in the school. I don't believe we'd better start the new year by kissing. That's the way French people all do. But then, my dear, if you ever went with another girl, a good girl and she didn't let you, you'd tell her I used to and you'd think I was a horrid thing. So please don't tease me anymore, will you dear? I know everyone thinks we do, but that's no reason why we should.

Goodbye dear.

P.S. Bring me a new stick of sealing wax, won't you please? Please write very soon.

December 27, 1904

Dear Laurence,

I'm oh, so happy. A week from tonight you'll be here. I was awful glad to get that spoon. I don't wonder that you could think of nothing more suitable. It's a beauty. I saw the little rustic bridge that we stood on before I read the note. The family ("Pa & Co.") is jealous because my spoon holds more sugar than theirs do. Thanks so much.

I have sealing wax for a lifetime. Guess you want me to write mighty often. Do you notice that I'm not writing with my fountain pen? It's with the dearest little teeny pearl handled pen that just came out of a brand new red plush case. Kitten Whitman sent it. I've got a dear desk. I got so many things for Christmas. Let me count 'em.

1. desk
2. spoon
3. pen
4. sealing wax
5. lamp mat from Nettie
6. a beauty of a pin cushion from Bessie
7. a cute little pencil from Art Bailey
8. bottle perfume from Carl in a little telephone
9. Poodle sent me his picture through the mail
10. Dan gave me a big box of Bon Bons
11. Ruth sent me a picture.

Mr. Romdenne must think I'm awfully particular to think I would not like that watch. I like it better because it is roman gold. I like it better than any I have ever seen.

Leslie showed me a picture of two little boys going fishing that he said he'd give me for Christmas. Tell him I'm waiting patiently for it. I don't know if he does act that way with other girls. It seems to me he doesn't. Of course, I'm just a very simple French girl. But someday, I'll have him understand that I'm not any old girl he can say any old thing to. Good land! I can tell him more about himself in five minutes than he can forget in a lifetime.

I wish that fine music would float clear to Elk River. I'd like to hear it. Why, Laurie. You can phone to me. I have two phones in my room. The one you gave us, and the one from Carl.

Come anyway, we'll fix it. Pa & Co. are going to Grandpa's, and I've persuaded Ma to trust you and me alone for an hour or two. They'll be here by four o'clock. I hate to stay all alone in that house in the forenoon, but they start off at ten in the morning so it will only make three hours. I'll have to be all alone, not enough time to get scared in. Please come early because when I get my work done, I'll surely be afraid. I can't read or do anything when I'm alone. You must write to me before you come. I'm awful anxious.

Goodbye.

December 28, 1904

Dear-Dear,

I got two more presents tonight, two needle books from Mabel Moores and Anna Murphy. Awfully pretty and useful too. Silly and Blanche came over to see us today but Anna had gone to Mrs. Herrick's to learn how to make Laurie's next Christmas present. It's something in drawn work, but you and your whole tribe can't guess what it is. I'm going after Ruth and Bessie Saturday. Ma is going to do some cooking at Grandpa's and I'll do the work and cook. So, whatever we have to eat Sunday will be what I did the day before. Won't you like that? I wouldn't do it for anyone else probably.

Mrs. Herrick, an Otsego neighbor.

It's snowed so we can't go in the woods unless you want to wear Pa's rubber boots. We can get our own supper if we run out of something to do. What do we care if there is not a thing to do, just so you're here?

I must retire. Be sure and come early. Joe has decided he wants to stay with me Sunday. Write immediately. Don't change your mind and put off coming. Can't wait until you come.

Glory, it's got to be Christmas again. It seems only a little while since I was doing up measly little packages last year.

I send you this little thing as a Christmas gift, but don't look at it closely. Please don't let anyone come within a mile of it because your sisters must be fine embroiderers. I never did it before in my life and never had anyone to initiate me into the difficulties of embroidery. This bag isn't finished to my satisfaction, and it doesn't look anything like the one I made a mental picture of, but it's the very best I could do without a gold or silver thimble. And I worked on it two whole Sundays. Perhaps the fact that I disgraced the Sabbath so, accounts for the poor work.

Anna Delia is the most happy possessor of a new, new desk. In consequence, thereof, she will be expected to write better letters hereafter, I'm thinking. It's got one big drawer down below, a little mirror on top, and inside there's the dearest little pigeon holes. They make me think of those in our brains, little places divided off to put chemistry and civics in. And, another little place to poke away happy thoughts when they suddenly pop into our cranium during Civics recitation. Do you remember the time in German I? Isn't it fun to think of our halcyon days?

Oh yes, and in with these pigeon holes, there's the dearest little drawer where I keep my pennies. Oh, it's a dear! Ma gave me a cup and saucer. My, I wasn't supposed to write a thing here, but oh, dear, I was so very happy I simply could not keep all this until I wrote a real letter.

Be sure to come on New Year's.

January 2, 1904

My dear,

I always feel so lonesome after you go away, that I must write to you. I hope you got home safely last night. The boys were staying up so as to take you home when you got ready. The horse was all harnessed and the boys expected to take you home. I'm awfully sorry. Next time, we'll depend on them.

I spent a lovely day with Grandma today. You ought to hear Ma tell the things Grandma told her about me. She seems to think I am so awfully good; almost angelic. She says I ought never to have any trouble, and she always had an idea that I would become a Catholic sister. The only reason I can see for her thinking that, is that she knew when I was little, I used to pray for hours at a time. Don't worry though. Good Land! It makes me try to be good when she thinks so much of me; I'm afraid I'm not what she thinks I am. She knew me when I was little, but I've changed.

I was disappointed, my dear, when you said you didn't expect to save another $100 by July. Won't you please, dear. It will be lots easier this time. See if it isn't. It took you only about five months to save that last; you have seven months to save another in, and you don't have to save any for Christmas money. That would be doing very well, if you could save $200 a year. Better than most young men. I'm... proud of you, too. Guess I'll ring off for tonight.

Au revoir,
Anna

January 4, 1905

I went over town this morning to see Ruth off. Got my old white hat (that you seem to like so well) trimmed. Guess that was all I did over there. I sew and read chiefly during vacation. I wish I had some good book to read.

I remember that last year you wrote something like this to me: "Resolved, that after Jan. 1, 1904, LAD will never speak a harsh word, or be cranky in any way, shape or manner to his Anna Delia." Wasn't that it? You kept it very, very well, my dear. I hope you can go on as well next year with this old resolution. And with that new one, too, please.

Laurie dear, don't get discouraged, will you, dear, 'cause you know you are doing very well, and will come out alive sometime. Everyone has troubles and I suppose they are good for us. Don't work too hard. Please save another $100.

Write soon to Anna

Note: Later that evening Anna and Laurence appear to have become engaged to be married.

January 9, 1905

I'm sorry, oh dear, so sorry that you have such an awful cold. Please be careful and not take more cold because gracious, I can't lose you, dear. I wish I could be there to bathe your eyes for you. Wouldn't they feel better? Dear, I'm so sorry! Don't you suppose it was from that "tempestuous ride?".

I have been feeling mighty blue since I sent that letter in which I said that I had succeeded in getting Mama to trust us alone. I took it the same as you did, but I'm positive Ma didn't mean that. She thought, and I agreed with her later, that it would be kind of funny if some of the neighbors should drop in and find us alone. Also, I was afraid to stay alone in the forenoon. And then the folks at Grandpa's would have asked if I wasn't going. What kind of a girl do you suppose they would've thought I was?

And what would they have thought of a mother who would leave her daughter alone with a boy. You can see that it wasn't quite proper. Mama trusts me because she has brought me up and she knows you are a gentleman because I told her you were. You won't feel bad about it anymore, will you dearest? Please don't 'cause it's bothered me awfully. I feel better now.

I take a great long walk every day to blow the cobwebs off my brains. I had a sleigh ride today. I think of you all the time I am out and wish you could be out with me. Yesterday, the "Fournier Brothers" hitched themselves to a hand sled and gave me a mighty swift ride over half a mile of pure, clean, white snow, clear past Corrows and back.

The Fournier Brothers, though not full brothers, were also cousins.

I don't object to your going bowling, dear. If you like it, I don't want to keep you away. I almost feel like going myself. Guess I will when school begins; all the other girls go. It must be fun. How can you think that you bother me? Of course you are a privileged personage. You know, dear, that I would do almost anything for you except let you kiss me for a while yet.

The boys would chop their heads off if you told them to. Pa and Mama like you too. They can see that you are doing better than those other boys in Elk River who don't work after they get through school. You can see for yourself that if you bothered me, I'd told you not to come on New Year's.

The counsel of love.

Please do not doubt that I love you any more, Laurence! I have always said that I would never promise to marry a man unless I loved him almost to madness. Surely, my dear, you do not think I am so ignorant as to pretend I loved you or just wanted to play at love. Love is a sacred thing to me as it is to you. If I had not cared for you, I could easily have gotten rid of you and played with another who could take me to everything and not wait until you came once in six weeks. I hope you'll reason as I do, and be satisfied.

I sometimes get out of patience and decide that you don't care for me. But there is no reason why I should think you don't. You actually thought a little prayer, dearest. Didn't it help you? I get more help and comfort from praying than from anywhere else. That's when I ask for help so that I can help you. I wish you'd try it. I'm not the least bit afraid you will get to drinking. It seems to me almost wicked to think of your doing such a thing. Yes, dear, I do try awfully hard to "be a good little girl for Laurie."

Oh, you called me a woman this time. It sounds strange, but good land, I'm 19. Can't you come pretty soon? I can't stand it six weeks, sure.

I hope you'll get over your cold soon. Take such good care of you that you can't help but get well and keep cheerful. Don't mind that eleven dollar bill; you won't notice that at all, and it will be such a relief to think it is paid. You'll try to save another $100? Please!

It's nine o'clock. Clara Waterman must be Clara Walters by this time. Last night I was alone with my brothers and I was so nervous that I put my watch, pen and two spoons under my pillow so that if the house burned down I'd have my dearest valuables ready to take away. I couldn't save piano and desk.

Wasn't it nice for both of us to get a letter the same day? I don't think we act very bad for an engaged couple, do you?

Au revoir.
Anna Delia.

January 14, 1905

Dear Laurence,

I've called you Laurie for so long that it seems funny to call you the other.

This is the last day of vacation, for which I'm pretty thankful.

My, I've been lonesome these last two weeks. I was so busy before Christmas that when I suddenly landed here with nothing I had to do, I just about died. Only one more month of hard work and then I can sew to my heart's content. I'm finishing a pretty violet pillow now, and then I'll make my graduating outfit myself.

Next time we drive to Dayton, bring your field glass, won't you please? We could see halfway across the earth from the top of that church. I must study now. I slept an hour this afternoon so I won't be able to sleep tonight and might as well study. I'm as happy as a big sunflower.

Sizing up Seniors of '05

Sing a song o' six pence, pocket full of rye,
Less than twenty seniors baked in a pie;
Dignified and proper, but don't behave at all.
Won't they make a dainty dish to set before Herr
Stahl?

January 20, 1905

My dear Laurence,

I must write to you tonight although I don't feel like it. Who would, when Grandma is awful sick. Ma is living down there. Pa sits with his head in his hands—lovesick, I guess. Ma has never left him over night for nine years. I have to do the work and go to school. Oh, it's a deplorable condition we're in.

Ma has just come home so I can have my party Saturday night. Grandma is better. It isn't a party that is all my own. The Juniors and Seniors got up a sleigh riding party and I asked them to our house for an oyster stew.

I had a lovely time at the party. My, you ought to have seen the dress. All the girls wore big kitchen aprons. We danced, chiefly. I fell flat once with Earl Martin.

Dan took me clear home. Guess he'll never take me anywhere again. I don't blame him. It was mean of me to make him go so far, but I don't care. I don't want to go anywhere anymore. I'm getting old.

I think I'll wait until you come to explain why we can't indulge in "even if we are promised." Too long to tell here.

No, dear, I won't go bowling if you don't like me to. I couldn't be hired to go. But it's no worse for girls than it is for men.

I wasn't angry about the ride but it hurt my feelings frightfully. Of course you're forgiven always. But I think that if it happens very many more times, I'll have to send back the little ghost ring. I'm afraid I will. I take that back, please. If it was anyone but Lucille I wouldn't care. You can take anyone else but her.

Of course we understood when we agreed on keeping that ghost ring and no one else need to know. Oh please don't propose, we'll pretend you have. I'd die.

Proposals are all right for novels. Let's not have a ring just now. The one we have now will suffice. We don't want anyone to know, do we? Wait until my hands get fleshier and nicer. I never cared much for rings. There's only one that I really want and two more that I like. Those three I'll have someday. A little tiny diamond set down in the ring. I like a certain kind of band ring and a minute graduating ring. Only those three that I'm dying to have. I guess you can kiss my picture goodnight. I kiss yours.

Laurence, next time you come, will you bring me Webster's Academic Dictionary? Like those black cloth bound ones we have at school, I think they're $1.50. I can't afford more than that. You must come soon 'cause I need that awfully. We're reading Hamlet.

Good Land! I can hear Pa call Ma his poor little girl. Really they are the spooniest. This morning he said he wouldn't want a little wife like me. Ma immediately took my part and asked him how he'd like one like Aunt Kate (200 lbs). Oh, he didn't like her; he wanted one just the size of Mama.

*"Spooniest"—
kissing and
hugging.*

She was just right. She weighs thirty pounds more than I do, but I can wear her things. I'm glad Leslie thinks I'm getting fatter. I'll get pretty if I don't watch out. But I'm getting paler and I've got circles around my eyes. But then all Fourniers have them, Pa and Co.

I was sick last Sunday. First time in five years that I had to eat in bed. Yesterday, Mr. Stahl asked me, "Well, Anna, how are you these last few days?" I told him I was very well, but was mighty sick last Monday. He was awful sorry and wanted to know what I was sick about. I guessed it was cold. He thought I'd eaten too much turkey on Sundays.

He's strange. He knows we'll have a bridge after I graduate when I won't need to walk across the river. He said so in Civics and made my face red. Mr. Norval and I have lots of fun talking French together. He can talk as well as I can. Doesn't have to stop to think a bit. Fine.

Au revoir.
Anadelia.

P.S. The Man will wonder why I haven't my Chemistry. I should have been studying. Guess he won't scold though. We're making nitrous oxide (laughing gas) and all of us are kept mighty good natured. I might send you some, I think you need it.

Farewell,
A.D.F.

Fun on the Elk River.

February 15, 1905

Dear Laurence,

Blanche has just told me that she was going down to see you, and she seemed mighty anxious to tell you something about me, so a bright idea struck me and I decided to write you a little something.

Daniel is going to take me to a party tonight. It's another poverty party but it doesn't happen to be on March 13. Perhaps won't be as eventful. I wish you could be here, especially when it's going to be that particular kind of party.

The lady has been seized with a burning desire to go to college. That's all, absolutely all I think about lately. But even if I do think a lot about that, I don't forget that you've owed me a letter for the last few months, it seems!

Art Bailey is watching the clock for me and every other minute he turns around and reminds me that I'll have to ring the bells in just so many minutes. He wants me to say, "Ditto." Must go and ring bells.

Au revoir.
Anna

March 3, 1905

Charles Wheaton told Bennie a lot of truck about you and asked a lot more. He said, "You don't know who I am, do you?"

"No."

"I'm Laurence's brother."

Bennie said, "Perhaps Charles has a brother named Laurence, but then it must be you." There is only one Laurence that Bennie knows.

One day, Walter Matson threw some bread crusts at me. I got mad and you ought to hear Nettie tell what I did. I took a good hold in his long hair with my left hand and slapped him on the head as hard as I could—eight blows. It didn't hurt him, of course, but my fingers immediately commenced to swell and my hand ached all day. It tires so easily now that I can't write.

Laurence! This is what Alta told the Literature class! "I'm very much pleased with your work. Your class work was good and you did well with that examination. Anna gave me an absolutely perfect paper and others of you did well."

You know those three finals I took. I got: Arithmetic, 72; English History, 87; and Civics, 91. I don't care about arithmetic 'cause not many got high marks. In history I was about the highest, and in civics only Effie B. and Albert Hill got 97 and 98 respectively. Carl and Harold got 90, Fred and Silly 82.

Au revoir,
Anadelia

March 10, 1905

Dear Laurence,

It was impossible for me to mail that letter so that you could get it on Saturday. I'm awfully sorry. I had to put it in another envelope so that you'd get it quicker.

I'm waiting for the men to come to breakfast and am pretty sleepy. Three o'clock every morning is get up time.

I've got some jim dandy biscuits for breakfast. I made some Monday and Uncle Fred said they were fine. Bennie said they tasted like cake, and Joe ate six, so they weren't bad. First I ever made.

Next day they didn't float in air, but they might have floated in thick milk, if it was thick enough to hold up a boulder. These last would float in air if it wasn't raining today. I wish I didn't have to get any more than you eat. I had good pancakes and strawberry sauce yesterday morn. I tell you I'm getting to be an expert!

I dreamt that Mama had come home, two nights in succession. They're coming.

Goodbye,
Deacon

March 28, 1905

My dear Laurence,

I must answer your letter tonight if I must mail it Thursday. Laurence, when you forget to mail my letters that way, please don't tell me about it. I'm living in pleasant anticipation of the lots of letters I'm going to get every Monday.

I wouldn't have cared much if Susan had read that last letter. Of course, you may bring Miss Dare over on Feb. 25, it's Silly's birthday. She won't invite me to supper. I have ceased speaking to her since last Friday.

Pray, why couldn't you come Sunday, even if you did come Saturday? You can and you must (if you can.) I had planned on your taking me to my cousin's on that day. She lives two miles below Dayton. I wanted to go after her wedding veil to use in the play. I have no way of getting it unless you take me out there. I depended on you. But if you can't, I suppose I'll have to be married without a veil. Can't you?

You would just about die to stay there at the Bailey's all day long and know that I was at home alone. Sunday is a lonesome day in the country.

Will they take partners Feb. 24? I suppose so. Otsego people do. If they don't, I can't go. If they do, we can take our horse, English Literature, same as before, if you want to.

The pond is called "the Pit" today. It was formerly a lake in Elk River and later a pond. The pond had been filled in and was used for school sports all year around before it was made into a stadium by the WPA in the 1930s. In 1905 it was just back of the Elk River school between Main Street and Fourth Avenue. Today it is next to Handke School and is being renovated by the Elk River Rotary Club and renamed Elk Hi Stadium.

School note written to Anna

April 20, 1905

Friend Anna,

Miss Dunn said that there were some sneaking boys in school. She meant Albert and I for going down to the pond that day. Miss Howard saw us and taddled. We explained matters to her this noon and she thought it wasn't so bad. I hope that you will be well enough to come to school tomorrow.

Your friend,
George A. Bailey

April 22, 1905

Dear Laurence,

I'll read you the play if you come Sunday, the 26th. I'll be awfully disappointed if you don't come. Of course, Mr. F. will let you be literary critic. I want you to come.

Effie Brown told me that eleven years ago today, when in the third grade, you and she were postmaster and mistress. You were chosen to deliver the valentines to the kids.

It was Dan who started to call me Topsy. Really, I think the name just fits me. I'm always so noisy. I call him Dixie. He calls me Frenchy, too.

Last week Charles W. answered the phone at Dickey's. Someone wanted Dan. Charles told Dan that Jim Cluto wanted him. Dan walked up there and he says, "Hello, you old stiff." It wasn't Jim, however, but Mr. Stahl! I think I'd have explained. He didn't. Dreadful.

Yes, I will be your Little Girl always except in the play.

Au revoir
Anadelia

Mr. Featherstone, acting editor of the Sherburne County Star News, offered Laurence the job of "literary critic" to cover the school play in which Anna starred.

April 23, 1905

My dear Laurency,

Dear! Indeed we did have some nice times during the last month. You can't imagine how I miss your coming at noon and evenings. It was just a week ago today that I was sick and you read to me. I'm not quite well yet, so you'd better come and read "somorum".

Oh, dear! I had the nicest time that day. You were feeling good, too, weren't you? I think you ought to come once again before you go to Walker.

I never prayed so hard in all my life as I did last night. At 1:25 A.M. I woke up to hear Pa say, "What do you want? You'd better take your horse and go."

I thought my time had come. Finally a man spoke from the buggy. He spoke French. He had been drinking and went to sleep so his horse came to our house and stopped by the windmill. He said he'd lost his way. So Pa told him he could put him on the right road and he said, "Alright, Uber." He's a young married man who lives where I told you Dayton used to be. His name is Goodin. He'd be an awfully nice man if he didn't drink.

We got our paper on Thursday this time. It was a pretty good example you set the Star News people. They do things on time now. Land! My hair is curly haute. I wish it would rain every week.

Well, I must go byebye. You must write as soon as you get to Walker.

Au revoir
Anna

Uber *is how Hubert sounds in French.* Hubert *is the French word we pronounce Hyoo-bear.*

Haute *means "very" in French.*

Anna's diary: Graduation

May 5, 1905

Dear, dear Laurency,

It's too bad about that job. I think Farley might help you. You'll find a better job than that, where you don't have to pay board and you'll save lots of money and we'll build a little cottage like that you saw.

They commenced on our bridge last Monday. Don't worry, dear, we'll come out alright. I think your father might give you a printing business of your own. We give our boys a farm as soon as they are able to run it and you ought to have a printing shop. You can run it. You'd make twice the wages than by working by the day and for others.

Of course, Anna's photo returned the kiss. Art and Fred make me awful mad. They sit and stare at me and tell each other how pretty I am as they make the other boys say I am, and they call me "Pretty," and "Dolly," right out in the street.

O dear. I do so want Laurency to come. I want Laurency all the time. Please write soon. I can't write a good letter when you tell me to. You'd better "take my idea." A man was praying and couldn't put his head full of thoughts into words so he said, "Lord, take my idea." You know what I want to say. Write soon.

G.B.D.

Editor's Note

In the summer of 1905, Laurence had jobs as editor
for the Motley Mercury and at Little Falls. In October,
he was at the Crookston Journal, and a month later at
Faribault. Arthur Dare in Elk River quoted an item by
his son in the Star News:

To a female subscriber who wrote that she was very
tall and wished to know how to neutralize the effect of
her height, the Crookston Journal offered this bit of
comforting advice: "Marry a preacher or an editor
and you will be short all the time."

In June Anna began attending St. Cloud Normal
School to earn a teaching degree or certificate, and by
1906-1907 held at least one teaching position. She and
Laurence continued to correspond from greater dis-
tances over the next two years, as she indicated in her
little diary. Unfortunately, none of those letters was
preserved among the attic memorabilia.

Anna's brief notes show that she lived off campus at
St. Cloud, travelling back and forth to Elk River quite
frequently, most likely by buggy or train. She stayed
in the old home of Mrs. MacGregor, a kind woman
who rented many rooms to college girls up to the 1950s.

Letter to Laurence from his mother

June 23, 1905

Dear Lad,

You ask how I liked Anna. Really, Laurence, I liked her very much indeed, and think that she seems like a very modest, lady-like girl, and so do we all. I am so glad I asked her down. I liked her ever so much better than the bold, silly kind like a good many of those Elk River girls. You will know to whom I refer without naming names.

"Those Elk River girls."

I think, as Daphne says, that it was putting Anna in a rather difficult position to come down here to see us in St. Paul, knowing we would be apt to criticize her, and I think she was quite brave to come. How did she like us, or didn't she tell you?

I must not forget to tell you that Papa went to Elk River Tuesday, and went to dinner at the Baileys', and they asked him about Miss Fournier's being down here, and he stood up for her to them, and told them she seemed like a nice young lady as he ever saw, and a good deal better and more modest than we had ever seen.

Now, Lad, I am telling you all this out of simple justice, and because I am afraid I have misjudged Anna in the past, and she seemed so different from what I had feared, but I still want you to be just boy and girl-friend: two "chums," as Papa said you seemed like, or two children together, as you said the time you went to Anoka.

With love as always,
Mamma

Letter to Laurence from his mother

June 28, 1905

Dear Laurence,

It is a beautiful morning, and I am sitting on my favorite porch to write to you.

Speaking about Anna being afraid to come down here that Sunday, I think it must have pleased her to have me invite her to come and get acquainted with us, almost enough to make up for disappointment in her house plans, shouldn't you think so? You did not say in your letter how Anna liked us. You know I asked you but perhaps she did not express an opinion. I am sure we all tried to be pleasant to her.

I think Anna has a rather odd voice, did you ever notice it, and somewhat of an accent, which makes her seem different from us, at least on first acquaintance. But I suppose a person would become accustomed to that.

Daphne said that Anna told her, going down to the depot that day, that she considered and reconsidered about coming down here, whether or not it was perfectly proper for her to do so, but of course it was. She came to see us, and not you alone, as she told Daphne. I knew it was about the only way for us to become acquainted with her, as I hardly ever go to Elk River, and would not be apt to meet her if I did.

With love as always,
Mamma

Laurence's response to a letter from his father

October 28, 1905

I just received a letter from Papa. So far it looks good for the job in Faribault, I may even get a place of my own. Oh – how Anna would love it! I hope I have a chance at making it on the daily and weekly paper at ten or even twelve dollars a week. Papa claims the owner of the paper is delighted with my description so far – based on what he told him. Hopefully he won't judge this book by the cover! Papa also said he doesn't want me running to Elk River every week or so. But how I do miss Anna, even for a day! My heart yearns to be with her, but how do I go about proposing! And what would Mama say?

Elk River Grade School and High School behind present-day Handke School
(about 1905-1910).

Letter to Laurence from his mother

November 7, 1905

Dear Lad,

Don't you believe you had almost better give it up there at Motley first or last, and come home until you can get another position? Somehow I feel so anxious over the idea of your having nothing but a cold room to stay in in this cold weather, that it almost makes me feel sick. I am so afraid you will take cold and get sick. As far as coming home often is concerned, you know you can never come often enough to suit me, and you know what Papa meant, not that he did not want to see you, but about going to Elk River and Otsego so often, that was what he meant.

Papa came back from Duluth yesterday morning. He brought me a lovely souvenir spoon showing the aerial bridge in the bowl.

The souvenir spoon is still in the house to this day.

Uncle Wesley Featherstone had a chance last week to get a job in the Pioneer Press manufacturing department at $18.50 per week, but he does not want to leave Elk River on account of Aunt Gertrude's health. Susan thought maybe she could get the place, but Papa says they do not employ girls there.

With love as always,
Mamma

November 24, 1905

My dear Laurency,

You can imagine how I wanted a letter from you, when I tell you I was about to phone your mama to find out if you were dead or alive or just barely either. Laurence, it's beastly for you to work so hard. I can't bear it. Just wait until next year.

Did you "kill the fatted calf" Sunday? Was your Ma disappointed or didn't they expect me? Ma couldn't understand why you weren't coming back this way Monday; she was thinking all the time of Fargo instead of Faribault. I sulked and scolded and stormed all day Sunday. Cried, too. "I don't believe it hurts young men to work, but that isn't working, it's slaving."

If you go to bed that late, I don't suppose you have thought of Jesus very often. Please don't forget for Anna's sake. I'm sure it will help you. "Tell it to Jesus, he will carry you through." I am sure that every word of that is true. Are there nice young men there for you to go with? You won't go with the kind that go in saloons, will you? I know you won't, but tell me you won't, please. I must be certain.

I wanted to let you read Miss Dunn's and Nettie's letters when you came, but didn't have time. That visit was too short. I don't dare hope you will ever come again.

What did your mother think of our ring? Did you bring it with you? You can't imagine how I miss it. I feel lost sans it. I wish you hadn't taken it, when you were going for so long.

Sans *means "without."*

How can I write a long letter! You'll have lots to tell me. Tell everything. O, I wanted to ask you, are you sure your mother did not read my last letter. You didn't say. Tell me. If she did, don't forget to send it back to me, 'cause I don't remember what I said.

Anna took an interest in her dreams, often seeing them prophetically.

Last night, I dreamt that Miss Van Slyke made me stand up before Literature class and wound a little black snake around my left wrist and I kept saying, "Oh, it's so cold, such an ugly head. Oh dear, O-o-o dear."

Raining. Be good. Don't work so hard as to hurt yourself. Above all, don't get discouraged or lonesome. You know you have to stay there until January, 1907. Be sure to write a long letter Tuesday.

Much love,
Anna

Letter to Laurence from his mother

October 26, 1905

Dear Lad,

I was very glad to get Anna's and your nice little note the first of the week, and also your later letter which I received this morning.

Did you tell Anna that you told me about the little bloodstone ring? I have not told Papa yet, but wanted to. I am glad Anna was pleased with the cup and saucer.

With love as always,
Mamma

Letter to Anna from Laurence

December 28, 1905

A Peep into the Future. We see a neat little cottage set far back from the highway in a beautiful cluster of trees and surrounded by a lawn of green grass cut up here and there into flower beds where the blooms are showing above the grass. It is just before twilight and as we ascend the gentle slope toward the cottage we can see two young people sitting upon the step leading to the door. They are talking earnestly in low voices and she turns to him suddenly and smiles. Then she stops and grasps a twig, fallen from a tree nearby and writes something in the path in front of the step. He puts his arm around her and watches as she writes. If we could have looked over their shoulder unobserved we might have seen too.

A D F

L A D

They gaze silently at the ground for some moments. He says something to her (can you imagine what he says?) in a whisper and she looks up at him, blushing, and smiles.

He then lifts her up and they pass inside the humble cottage leaving us with thoughts of two hearts made one. We pause, and looking toward heaven offer up a silent prayer to God and thank Him for that which is called Love.

Finis

January 26, 1906

Laurence dear,

You were so pleasant and jolly and witty last Sunday. You looked so handsome; you noticed that I was watching you when you went to the house. What Laura said is true.

I didn't send that book to Leslie because you said I hadn't better. Am I not obedient? You comforted me so much, even if I couldn't say a word. How I longed to be with you the next day.

Dearest, that finger must hurt! Joe had one of his fingernails pulled right out. I was alone with him, too. I cut the skin around the nail and took it out.

Didn't you cry since you were five years old? I cry often. Our family is crazy and can't stand anything anyhow. One of Pa's brothers died when his wife died. I'm not supposed to tell that but we're all that way.

I feel lots better now that I have gotten a nice letter from you.

Au revoir,
Anna

P.S. I hope you can come before the strawberries are all gone. There are tons of them. I'm sure we could pick at least twelve quarts every day. I picked sixteen immense ones in about two square feet of ground. One of them measured five inches around.

Sherburne County Star News

February 15, 1906

Bridge Across the Mississippi River Between
The village of Elk River and Otsego

Country People Pour Into Town
and Make Merry

Saturday was a big day in Elk River. The morning opened bright and cold, 20 or more below zero but a large crowd came from all directions just the same, to see the new bridge and partake of the barbeque and get some bargains at the stores and at the auction. Probably the largest contingent came from Otsego. They carried a banner on which was inscribed "Elk River Annex."

They also indulged in several yells, the work of a local poet. The reporter only caught the words of one. It ran about like this:

"Hurrah for the beef! Hurrah for the liver!
Hurrah for the bridge!! That spans the river."

Jack Frost had something to say about where dinner should be served. He decreed that indoors was the only place. Consequently the Houlton store building opposite the Riverside Hotel was turned into a huge dining room, where the wants of the men were looked after while the ladies were being served in the hall where the music was.

There was no attempt at getting the people together for a set program; the weather was too cold for that outside and there is no room here that would accommodate such a crowd. The main thing was to show off the bridge. There was a big dance in the evening to celebrate the new wagon bridge.

The new bridge connecting Elk River and Otsego

As for the bridge, nothing but praise was heard for that beautiful structure.

The bridge was designed by C.A.P. Turner, of Minneapolis, one of the best engineers in the northwest.

The bridge cost $24,000 which was raised as follows:

State appropriation	$ 3,000
Village of Elk River	7,000
Town of Elk River	7,000
Town of Otsego	3,000
Wright County	3,000
Total	$24,000

For the benefit of former residents, it may be of interest to know that the bridge is about 200 feet down river from where the old H. Houlton saw mill used to be. The right of way for the street on the Elk River side was donated by N.K. Whittemore, that on the Otsego side by W.H. Houlton.

The bridge is a very sightly affair as seen from the cars as the train approaches town from the Twin Cities, the broad curve of the river making a handsome view possible. The channel is covered with a span 226 feet long, 35 feet above the water. This will make clear sailing for the Boom company's steamboat after about two feet has been removed from the top of the smoke stacks, and will prove much more satisfactory than a draw bridge would have been.

The old ferry which has been in service here so long it must be nearly 50 years ago that T.S. Nickerson put in the first boat will no longer ply the river, and the running logs and ice and the dark nights will no longer annoy or terrify those who have occasion to cross from one town to the other.

Susan's Journal

April 20, 1906

Anna, our sister-in-law-to-be came down to St. Paul to spend Easter Sunday with us. She is rather a nice little girl but she and Laurence seem like babies to a woman of mature years like me. I went to the depot to meet her, and as Laurence came from Faribault at seven, we had a musicale that evening. Easter Sunday Daphne and I went to People's Church with our new rigs on, and Laurence's friend, Mr. Hanson was here to dinner, which was a big spread. We had a livery rig in the afternoon and went way up Summit Avenue and had a fine ride. We took Daphne to the depot and came back and had another musicale. Anna went around with LAD all day Monday, and Wednesday he accompanied Anna home to the farm.

Mature years: Susan was almost two years older than Laurence.

Livery rig: rental buggy and horses.

Susan's Journal

September 20, 1906

The world still moves, and so do I. The scene of action has changed from The Wendell at 768 Cedar Street in St. Paul to a most beautiful and homelike residence at 632 Holly Avenue, on the hill. Yes, the impossible has actually happened and we have been enjoying the comforts of a house of our own for about three months.

I had a week off, and we four girls—Laura Bailey, May Wheaton, Daphne and Susan Dare—took a river trip down the Mississippi River to Wabasha on the steamer Cyclone. It was a delightful trip and we had a jolly time together. The boat stopped ten minutes at all the largest towns including Hastings, Red Wing, Lake City, Prescott, etc.

Laurence has changed his location and is now reporter for the Duluth Evening Herald. He actually admits that he likes both the town and his work, so there is hope.

I am still donating my worthy services to the West Publishing Co. and am still on the ragged edge of leaving, as usual. Daphne has gone back to teaching kindergarten at Superior, and quiet reigns supreme in this household.

The great Minnesota State Fair was held here two weeks ago, and a bunch of West Publishing Co. girls, including me, went to view the fascinations of the Pike three nights out of six.

Sherburne County Star News

June 18, 1907

Popular young Couple
Married Tuesday Morning

The marriage of Miss Anna D. Fournier and Laurence A. Dare was solemnized Tuesday morning at the Dayton church, only the immediate families of the contracting parties being present. The bride was tastefully attired in an embroidered gown of white linen and carried a shower bouquet of white snow balls.

After the ceremony a wedding breakfast was served at the home of the bride's parents, Mr. and Mrs. Hubert Fournier, after which the bridal couple departed, via the Twin cities, for Duluth, where they will make their future home.

As the train pulled out they were lavishly showered with rice and old shoes and their trunks tied up with white streamers and well plastered with red hearts of all sizes.

Both of the young people are well known in Elk River and they carry with them the best wishes of a host of friends.

Laurence's Journal Entry

June 19, 1907

Yesterday was the happiest day of my life. It was the day I had been waiting for for many years. Anna and I finally got married! We'd put it off for so long and now it finally happened. I'll never forget that day.

It was perfect. An early morning service with both of our families there. Anna wore a beautiful embroidered gown made of white linen. Down the aisle she carried with her a bouquet of white snowballs. I was in my suit. We walked down the aisle of Dayton church, said our vows, and the priest pronounced us husband and wife.

Afterwards we went to Anna's parents' home for a traditional wedding breakfast. Soon after, we said our good-byes and were showered with rice as we got on the train. The train was all tied up with shoes, white streamers and plastered with red hearts of all sizes. We were on our way to our new home in Duluth, Minnesota.

Susan's Journal

August 10, 1907

I have been reading the preceding pages of this document and I perceive that one of the seven wonders of the world has been denied space in the pages of my diary. My little baby brother is married. Yes, really that's the truth, I don't wonder you are surprised. He and Anna actually took the fatal vows before the priest at the Dayton Church on June 18, '07.

Anna is a dear girl but I did hate to have Laurence get married. It makes me feel old enough to be married and out of the way, but we cannot always direct fate in those matters. They have gone to housekeeping in Duluth and are as happy as bugs in a rug.

Life Together

1908-1909

After a brief stay in Duluth, Minnesota, where Laurence liked to say of himself that his beat was covering the waterfront, the young couple had moved to North Branch before the year had passed. As they excitedly awaited the birth of their first child, Anna did not venture from home. She managed, however, with some help from friends and relatives, to keep up with the many burdens of household work, and to keep herself busy with sewing little things, gardening chores, reading, and most diligently praying for her child, her husband, and the little family which would become her whole interest and concern for many years.

She read the *North Branch Review* with interest since her young husband had become its editor and publisher. He was actually named in the masthead of the small town weekly as its owner and publisher, L.A. Dare & Co.

What this meant in subtle translation to L.A. Dare, was that his father Arthur Newman Dare of Elk River, publisher of the *Sherburne County Store News* since 1879, state representative to, and later Speaker of the House of Representatives in the 1890s, had managed to purchase the *Review* from Editor Bede on behalf of himself, AND, and son LAD.

Through the several years LAD and Anna spent at North Branch, Laurence made a success of his side of the business. As familiar as he had become with his family's S*tar News* in Elk River, he wrote editorial paragraphs about as well as his dad.

Arthur had enjoyed state-wide approval by most weekly editors around the state. (On his death years later, Arthur was affectionately described by one publisher friend as "the best paragrapher in the state.") Editorial positions tended toward agreement politically among the numerous Republican-leaning journals of the day. There were fewer journals in the liberal camp, but strong views and high form kept readers alert as they scanned editorials. Most publishers found their strongly-worded opinions added more readers, and the public had more to talk about.

Letter from Anna to her mother-in-law, May, shortly after moving to North Branch

December 1908

Dear Mother Dare,

You will probably be greatly surprised, but I tho't it would be better to tell you before I went that there is going to be a little Laurence about next June.

Will it be embarrassing to you and the family to have me come? If so, I will send Laurence alone, although he says he will not go without me.

Of course, you can tell the girls, but I would rather it would not go any farther, so please warn them accordingly.

Lovingly,
Anna

Letter from May to Anna

December, 1908

Dearest Little Girl,

I was so surprised and pleased and proud when I received your note, and have been thinking about the wonderful news ever since; and what a beautiful, holy thing it is. As to your questions about being embarrassing to have you come, no indeed, of course not, and if Lad comes without you, I will send him right back after you. You must remember he wouldn't enjoy it himself to come alone.

When I read your note, I felt quite "compunctious," as we say, to think I had not managed to get over to visit you, as you had urged me to do, but can only say that I never suspected there was any special reason why you wanted it, and now, as we will see each other now anyway, I think I will try to plan for a nice visit with you sometime after Christmas.

We were glad to get your Christmas list, and when I write Friday perhaps I will enclose a copy of the family list, just for you both to laugh over. Remember May Dare does not want any big presents this year, as Santa Claus is quite hard up at this end of the line. Tell Laurence he will probably get his automobile. I suppose nothing less than a "Packard" would fill the bill.

Now, Little Girl, be sure and come. Just you hold your head up and don't be bashful and everything will be all right. I have not told the girls the secret yet, for I did not know whether you would rather I would or not.

Goodbye for this time, dear
And a kiss from Mamma May

Letter from Anna's dear school friend, Mabel Moores

February 25, 1909

My dear Anna,

I hope you will pardon my delay in answering your dandy letter. Don't you ever think I am not interested in your household duties, etc. I can just imagine you bustling around in a big apron and those pretty brown curls done up on top of your head. I would like to step in and have a good old fashioned chat with you some morning.

Say, Anna, next time you write, tell me about the inside of your house and what cute things you have, because I know you must have some because you received so many presents (either wedding or shower).

Do you hear from Nettie T. any now? I wonder how she is. I would certainly like to see her. Do you hear from many Elk River folks? I only hear from Bernice. I have had one letter from Selma and one from Mrs. Bert Gilcrest. The principle news for me is the *Star News*. Mrs. Fletcher sends that to me every week. I suppose you knew the Fletchers had moved to Worthington. They have been gone nearly five weeks now. I miss them terribly but hope to survive until spring. Do you ever hear from Bessie, and how does she like her work? I hear Alice Beck was teaching 8th grade somewhere but don't know just where.

This week is examination week and that means work for me. I am rather proud of the work the children are doing; four out of six had 100 in Spelling examination today in second grade.

With oceans of love, I am
Sincerely yours,
Mabel G. Moores

Letter from Mamma, Mrs. A.N. Dare, to Laurence

May 5, 1909 Wednesday

Dear LAD,

We were all so surprised and pleased and proud when we got your telegram this morning and so excited ever since, we hardly know what to do with ourselves, but feel just like trooping over to North Branch in a body to see the new baby boy. Papa is just as bad as the rest and says he really has to go over on business. I say I have to, and really, Lad, I can't stand it 'till I see that baby. We really do mean to come soon. And that reminds me, I wanted to tell you if you should need me to come and help out, or anything, let me know and I will come.

Don't you worry or feel a bit anxious, Lad, for I am sure Anna is going to be all right, and too happy to be sick long.

I do hope you have help in the office by now, but if not, never mind; no one will expect much of a paper under the circumstances. I am so glad it is a boy, so you can call him Daryl, as planned.

I will say goodbye for this time, with love as always
For Lad and Little Girl
And the Little Lad,
Mamma

P.S. Papa says he is going to put in a remembrance to help out.

May's Prayer for Little Lad

May 5, 1909

The angels whispered in Heaven,
"A baby goes today."
"Let us pick one of our fairest souls,
To speed on its earthward way."

Give to the new soul courage,
To ever stand for the right.
Send a soul that is humble
In the gracious Father's sight.

Give him the gift of gladness,
O Father who rulest all,
Then he shall not faint or falter.
He will stumble but will not fall.

A precious power, O lend him
To prove that Thy love is true,
To show by example to others
A hope that is ever new.

And the best of all gifts give him
A faith that is clear and true
When the ills of life assail him,
A faith that shall carry him through.

Letter to L.A. Dare from Mamma

May 7, 1909 (Friday morning)

Dear Lad,

It seems as though I can hardly think of anything these days except for the little Family at North Branch. I keep wondering all the time just how you are getting along. I was so glad to get your note the day of the telegram, as it told more details, and it relieved our minds greatly to hear that the doctor said the prospects were all of the best. I suppose Anna's Mother is with her now, which will of course be pleasant for both of them.

When we first got your telegram that morning, Papa telephoned the name up to me, and I was so pleased I had to immediately call up Aunt Gertrude, and Aunt Lill, and Susan, and they were all very much surprised, especially Gertrude, as she had not heard anything about it at all. Then Harriet arrived from the south that afternoon, and she also was duly surprised at the news. She said when she went away, the last she heard, Anna was on the eve of giving a big party. That was a slight exaggeration, of course, but I told her how bright and well Anna had been all winter.

We are having a few improvements made around the house, and things have been rather torn up and uncomfortable for several days. We have been house-cleaning for one thing, and having the floors varnished, and now the porch is being screened in . . .

If you manage after awhile to get a good man in the office, that you can trust to get along alone, won't it be nice if you and Anna and the Little Lad can come home and spend a few weeks. . . I think it would do you good to have a little rest, and you could write editorials and send them over from here.... Think it over, won't you? Tell Anna I don't believe Daryl would cry on the train.

My cold still hangs on, with a disagreeable, hacking cough, but nothing serious. It has kept me from driving out, though, and our poor horse Starlight needs exercise. Probably Starbright will not go quite so much now, either.

I will say goodby for this time, with love as always for Lad and Little Girl and Little Lad.

Write more.

Mamma

P.S. Noon: Just received your letter, and very glad we were to hear a few details about the boy. I had not imagined he could be so big, coming so soon. Eight pounds, just what his father weighed. I am so glad all is going so well. Perhaps I will come over awhile. Did you get Papa's remembrance safely?

May 9, 1909

"The Grandchild," by May Dare

With sympathies deepened and sweetened,
And strengthened by life's changing mood,
And a gratitude youth never gave us,
With blessings not understood. . .

We look on the wee small nestling,
Straight from the angels he came.
O the beauty and glory and mystery,
And the darling bears our name.

A human soul, he lies there,
With journey but just begun,
May all blessing rest upon him,
Dear little son of our son.

A page from Anna's diary

May 11, 1909

After a short, sweet visit with us, our little son Daryl Dare, has gone to his own beautiful Home, with his own Heavenly Father. Born May 5, he was taken with a severe illness Saturday, and passed away early Sunday morning, May 9. The remains were taken to Dayton, Minnesota, for burial, and a short service was held there on Monday, May 10.

May 12, 1909 (Sunday forenoon)

Dear Lad,

I wanted to come with Daphne, hoping there might be some little thought I could do for you, but they all discourage my doing so for fear of getting sick, especially as my cold is so bad. Words are always inadequate at such a time, dear Lad, so I will not try to tell you two we all sympathize with you and Anna, but I know just how you feel, and how hard it is to bear. The only thing to do is to try to trust that God knows best, and be thankful that you still have each other.

Life will look bright to you again after awhile. I have been through it all, for you remember little Daisy.

If you or Anna would like me to come, or if it would be the slightest comfort to you, I could make the early train in the morning.

Mamma

May 14, 1909 (Tuesday evening)

Dear Anna,

I have just got to write tonight and tell you that Arthur did not show me your note until he got home from North Branch. The one you wrote Saturday. Had he done so, nothing would have kept me from going too, and Luann says she should have come also, to try to help a little. Dear Little Girl, I cannot bear the thought that you should think we were intending to neglect you by not coming. It was just simply that we did not know the circumstances. We thought from Laurence's letters that everything was going along so nicely, and that when you needed us you would let us know, as I told him to do, you know. I see now that one of us should have gone right away at first, but we did not know your mother was sick, and thought a little stomach trouble was all that ailed the little one.

I am so sorry. I do hope you are getting along all right now, and that you will be up and feeling well again before long. Don't be independent, though, and try to be up and around too soon, will you? Tell Daphne we miss her but are getting along all right, and we want her to stay as long as you need her.

Why didn't Laurence keep Arthur to help get the paper out so he could have it a little easier this week? Arthur said when he went away, he should probably stay until the paper came out. Goodbye for this time.

Love as always,
Mamma May

P.S. Dear Anna, you must keep up a brave heart, and get well for Laurence's sake as soon as possible.

P.P.S. Dear Anna, you know how much I sympathize with you, but I am trying to be cheerful.

Letter to Anna from her friend, Ruth Atkins

May 19, 1909

Soror dear,

I was so happy last week when I saw in the paper that your little one had come. I had been hoping that it was to be, and then I wanted to write to you right away, but I just couldn't. And now Betty tells me the other. I'm so sorry, dear heart, I wish I had you here where I could love you.

And yet I'm glad, so glad, girl, that the joy has come to you, if only for a little while. It's the highest and holiest joy in the world, I truly believe, and it is yours for all time now, dear. You have had the child and once being yours, he is always yours, and you can never lose him or forget. Someday his brother will come to you and you will be able to love him better and truer because of this first love.

God knows the why, dear, we don't, but oh, it is such a blessing to know He knows, and to know that no mistake can ever be, with His own hand to choose for me. There are so many things that your little one has been surely saved from, and so tho' it is hard for you, you know it is better for him and better for you in some way, or it would not be. He knows best.

I want you to come to see me this summer, Soror, to really let me see you. I've not had a chance since Laurence took you. I expect to be in Elk River all summer, and surely your folks can spare you for a little time. You don't want to forget that your old friends love you just as much as ever. Tho' you did go off and leave them, nobody blamed you, dear, but we love you too.

There are only two weeks more of real school, then state exams, then vacation. I would be glad if it weren't that I can't have these same children next year. They

Ruth Atkins and Anna were long-time friends. Both knew French and spoke it together. They called each other "soror," or sister.

are dears and I am actually almost glad that some of
them won't pass in everything and must come back to
me occasionally next year. We've had such good times
together.

Write to me when you can, Soror, just because you
are Soror and the only one I've got.

With Love,
Ruth E. Atkins

May 24, 1909

My dear Anna,

I have been thinking a lot about you lately. . . I heard of the loss of your baby and cannot tell you how sorry I am, but as you say, you still have Laurence, and Anna, you are so exactly fitted for a lovely mother that children will not be denied you.

Our school is over, or nearly over. We have just this week left, then are going to have finals all of next week. We are going to break up housekeeping and I shall board next year. Mamma is not well enough to keep house, so it will be better all around.

I was invited to sing at the Junior Reception up in Elk River, but as I am going to sing at the graduating exercises, and want to go up for the banquet, I decided not to go up. I am going to spend a week with Blanch in Anoka some time this month and have one or two other short visits to make. Then I'm going to Mankato to visit May Midell during July. In August I'm going to spend visiting Bucks who live about 75 miles out from Duluth. They have saddlers, drivers, a big machine, row boats, and a launch, maids, etc. so I always have a fine time when I go up there. If I can, I am going to stop off a day to see you on my way up. I'll bring some music with me. You will not know my voice, it has broadened and deepened so.

I told you that I belonged to the glee club, Enterplan Club it is called. Well, I have just been elected to the Alanthus Literary society. There are four societies and Alanthus has the most prominent girls in it. I am so proud. I did not join a sorority this year because Papa did not want me to, but I may another year. I hate to have school close in some ways, I am having such a good time, but my eyes are getting bad again and I am pretty well tired out, but the extensive visiting I have been doing and will do this summer will build me all up again, and I'll also have another year here to look forward to with pleasure. (If you cannot read this, please blame Mama and Jeanette, for they are talking to me, at me and around me, and I hardly know what I am writing, but my intentions are grand anyway.)

I hear Leslie Bailey is planning to come down here to school next year. Do you know anything about it?

It is now so close to finals that there is not much going on. Forty of us gave an opera called the "Mikado," which was the cutest thing. We had to practice so much for it that I could not do much else. The fraternities each give a formal dancing party. Usually a dinner dance at the Plaza Lafayette Club, Glen Morris or some such small place every spring. The man I am particularly interested in just now is a Sigma Chi, and that afternoon and evening we gave the "Mikado," they gave their formal. If I was not cross! I could have bitten a nail in two pieces. Of course he might not have asked me, anyway, but if he had not, I should have blacked his eye for him, or fisted him as you are always doing. He has a very pretty voice and just loves music, so we get along very well.

There was a May fete over at College Thursday afternoon and evening. They crowned the May Queen and danced the May Pole dance; each sorority had a booth to sell things, and in the evening the "U" Band played. They had tableaux, pageants, and another May Pole dance. In the evening, men danced it with the girls and it was so pretty. They wore white duck trousers and dark coats and were supposed to be the handsomest men in college because they were with the queen's maids.

Please let me hear from you. I am going to be a model letter writer this summer and next winter for boarding. You have lots more time.

With heaps of love,
Marguerite

P.S. Please give my regards to Laurence.

Anna's Diary

1914-1918

Anna was an orderly, conscientious person. She kept track of many day-to-day tasks, chores, and spiritual challenges. She was also a voracious reader and kept a small red leather notebook in which she listed titles and authors in long, neat rows. She kept track at different times in her marriage of concerts, plays, operas, and many other things which interested her.

Authors she had enjoyed included Louisa May Alcott, Nathaniel Hawthorne, Kipling, Irving, J.F. Cooper, Longfellow, Scott, Dickens, and George Eliot. Among her favorites were Shakespeare, Tennyson, and Longfellow.

The sampling of pages that follow from Anna's diary shows the rhythm and struggles of life before World War I, the challenges of being a good mother (Alan Dare was born in 1914) and wife, and Anna's determination and effort at making her life be a testimony to her spiritual convictions.

An entry from Anna's small leather notebook. The name of the book is on the left page, the corresponding author on the right page. At last count, Anna had read and recorded 278 books in this notebook.

1914

- Translated 64 lessons of English into French.
- Finished book of Sonatas: 78 hours
- Read carefully, "The Pathfinder's Sketch Book."
- Read "Nancy, the Joyous," "Strawberry Acres," "The Blunderer," "The Rise of Roscoe Payne," and "Pollyanna."
- Made a fireless cooker that works.
- Took leading part in home talent play.
- Made six pair curtains.
- Made an apron.
- I can make doughnuts!
- Sewing: new pink poplin dress, several madeovers, new white voile, one gown, two combinations, plush muff and collar, cuffs and buttons on winter coat.
- Memorized, "Nearer Home," "Emperor's Nest," "The Arrow and the Song," "The Immaculate Conception," by Father Ryan (47 stanzas).

Other historical events of 1914:

The Panama Canal opens for traffic August 15.

World War I begins.

The dial phone system is demonstrated in Minneapolis.

Will Rogers appears at the Orpheum Theater.

February 5, 1914

Lunched at A.N.'s

Dinner
  Spuds
  Boiled eggs
  Creamed macaroni
  Dutch cheese
  Apricot sauce
  Frosted cookies

Evening
  Prune tapioca
  "Cushions"
  Toasted marshmallows in evening.

February 17, 1914

I washed a pile of dishes.
Washed my hair brush.
Practiced an hour on piano.
Cut a lot of carpet rags.
Did up daily work.
Swept all carpets.
Cleaned myself up.
Got supper.
Washed all day's dishes.
Had French class.

February 18, 1914

Wrote one hour. I'd like every day to be full like these, when I am well.

Practiced piano an hour.

Cut carpet rags.

Righted rooms.

Changed bed.

Got dinner.

1916

January
- Marked breakfast cloth.

February
- Worked around sash cloth, shortened all baby's flannels, also four dresses, new necks and cuffs on two of them. Made over three white petticoats.

March
- Made pair of pillow cases with medallions.
- Made up two dresses from Mrs. Parson's gift.
- Made three petticoats for one-year dresses given to him.

April
- Made fancy bib for shower (Mrs. Prof. White), shortened flannels again. Six dresses. Sheet with medallion....

May
- Made new bedroom curtains.

June
- Made dish towel and marked it.
- Canned 12 pints of strawberries.
- Canned 6 quarts of blueberries.
- Had aluminum demonstration at house; 17 ladies.

August
- Made three outing gowns for son.

September
- Guest town crochet edges.

- Went to city weekly for $75 of tooth work, donated by brother Joe.
- Made baby dress and petticoat for shower for Bess Opitz.
- Afterwards, exhibited at Sherburne County Fair and placarded, "GOOD."
- Made fancy bib for Commercial Club Sale.
- Made three kinds of pickles, 8 quarts relish.

October
- Baked four loaves of bread every Monday.
- Doing family washing and ironing every week.
- Failed to finish three bluebird dollies planned for this year.
- Close to physical breakdown.

Other historical events of 1916:

Silent movies.

First golf course in Minnesota opened—the 6-hole Glenwood Golf Course, Minneapolis.

1st Minnesota Regiment of the National Guard called for Mexican border service.

The Elk River Livery and R.E. Dare purchase a new funeral car that replaces the hearse used since the "early days."

Star News installs an up-to-date linotype machine.

Big Lake City Ice Company enlarge ice house and employ 75 men.

Worst dust storm in county history—raged two days.

Electric street lights come to Elk River.

October 19 snowstorm dumps 5" of snow.

Elk River area receives new fire engine.

State law for new speed limits: 15 mph in village limits and 8 mph at intersections.

January 13, 1916

I began last night to strengthen my will after reading an article on the subject.

After the first day's effort I find these triumphs:

1. Kept STRENGTH constantly before my mind.

2. Didn't loaf.

3. Did lunch work promptly.

4. Refrained from reading the newspaper until after lunch work was out of the way. Tremendous effort, as Babe had to be put to sleep also.

5. Shut down on my beloved department, "Training the Child," and read it just at suppertime.

6. Cleaned and mended Laurie's suit; hateful task.

7. Nobly refrained to answer back when L. spoke sharply to "Hurry and take Babe, Great Guns."

8. Breathing exercises on opening window at bedtime.

   A. Cold Cream.

   B. Bending exercises.

   C. Kneel at bedside.

   D. Care for scalp.

January 16, 1916

Strengthen me for the trials that will come upon me today.

Keep me pure in heart, and true to my ideals.

Let me be done with fault-finding.

May I never be hasty in judgment.

Deliver me from the vice of egotism.

Oh, let me not forget to be kind.

I dressed in the cold. Spoke impatiently to Little Boy when he spilled a spoonful of mush.

Yielded to the mention of my slight headache.

Wasn't indolent today.

Ate much without sugar.

Ordered myself to stop eating candy and won't touch another piece of this supply.

Didn't read papers until dishes were done at noon and night.

January 17, 1916

One cup unsweetened coffee for breakfast. I don't seem to be doing anything remarkable, only the daily duties done promptly and cheerfully as I should have done them these last ten years. My habits have been lax.

Washed Babe's flannels and nighties and eight diddies.

Pressed L's suit.

Cleaned bathroom.

I am denying myself little things, but they straightway become easy as soon as I make up my mind.

January 24, 1916

"Become an expert at forgetting. The mind becomes quick and alert to remember only the things worth remembering. The mind is given to beautiful things, worthwhile things, and we must remember always that we are in the presence of God."

Be patient. Keep CALM and good natured.
Power is calm.
Justice is calm.
Knowledge is calm.
Ability is calm.
Mastery is calm.
"Be devout and calm and Jesus will abide with you."
In all verse about the moon, it always rides "calm and serene high in the sky."

Father, give the weary
Calm and sweet repose;
With thy tender blessings
May our eyelids close.

"Each soldier in battle has a CALM clear conviction that if he falls, he is going to enter into some life beyond" (Harry Lauder).
"May I grow CALM serene and gentle. Let me not forget to be kind."
Ben Hur calmly endured the gaze of the sheik.
"Without labor there is no coming to rest."
"My peace I give unto you. Let not your heart be troubled, nor let it be afraid" (Jesus).
At Benediction a peace comes over us that is not of earth, a CALM resignation which comes from intimate union with God.

February 1, 1916

Strong are the links and the bonds which confine my heart and soul to Thee, Jesus, all mine.

With thee is the principality in the day of thy strength. I had strength to silently endure two accusations that I made Alan scream for an hour. Rocked another hour.

"The only way to successfully STRENGTHEN the will is to prove to yourself that you are strong. To prove it to others is vanity."

That's the only thing that prompted me to take a cold shower this morning.

February 14, 1916

Red and white supper for Alan's year and a half birthday.

Year and a half birthday party.

Little Boy is 17 months old today. I did all my house work and cleaned up and dressed before touching the Sunday paper. Cleared up the house ready to brush up in morning as soon as Babe is dressed. Yielded once.

Red means Shame. Defended myself when accused of torturing Babe in cleaning his nose.

February 15, 1916

Evening of the third day. Still sticking to my household tasks. Satisfaction in having an orderly house. Refrained from reading the morning paper until after supper. Took off the glory of my victory by explaining that I nobly refrained in order to get certain work done, when Lad laughed at me for reading the morning paper in the evening. I lost patience waiting.

February 16, 1916

Stayed alone all night. Little Boy so restless that we were up from one o'clock to 4:30 A.M. I didn't say anything about it to anyone.

Talk health and you become healthy. Think and talk happiness and you acquire a sunny disposition (personal experience in 1907).

Keep STRENGTH constantly before your mind and you become STRONG in body and mind.

Avoided personalities: Mrs. Darrow's fingers, longest I ever saw. The loss of Mrs. Page's teeth.

Mabel Trask afternoon, dinner.

Callers: Lillian Erickson, Mrs. Page and Mrs. Darrow.

February 18, 1916

I lost my temper last night. Brought Alan down stairs three times before midnight. Spoiled child. Healthy as they make them! I made Babe a blue velvet coat with fur trimmings and quilted lining, with help from Daphne.

"You cannot hide your thoughts because they soon become your character." It requires strength of mind to turn on cold water after hot shower.

March 1, 1916

Spent day in city and it was some day, ending up with my getting on the wrong train and being bodily lifted off when the train was going at a pretty good clip.

I refrained from going into hysterics when besieged by crowd and question of, "Were you trying to get killed?"

Calls—Aunt Lil.
Sunday—Ben and Frank.
Arthur for dinner two days.

I have acquired enough strength of will to throw off a yoke of oppression! . . .

Susan said, "I don't know who is more self-willed than you are.

A note written by Anna in Alan's Baby Records

October 30, 1916

A mother washes clothes in the lowest regions of the river. Her mind is on the task at hand but her subconscious mind is on the fourteen-month old in the highest regions of the cottage. Three times a minute she pauses in her splashing and inclines an ear in the direction of the stars. Puts a bunch of little nighties to soak and all the time is getting more and more uneasy and working up a frenzy of anxiety for fear the Angel is awake and liable to creep off the bed. Or perhaps he has already landed on his caput and is tired out with screaming. Water doesn't run out of the hose fast enough. This little bit will have to do.

Mother tears up the stairs, across first floor, up another flight. Open the SW bedroom door. A pretty boy with one very pink cheek is awake. (Now I understand that part of the song, "Like a baby that just has awakened.") So warm and soft and firm those round cheeks. He is bewildered at the pile of covers from which he has partly extricated himself. Mother must take up the boy: Joy, joy, joy! Baby volunteers a warm, humid, open mouthed kiss and is carried down stairs.

A boy immediately spies something new and red. Mother and Baby must examine it and feel cautiously in case it's hot. It isn't hot. (We are always afraid something new is going to be hot, because some new things like an oil heater and electric receptacle are hot.)

1917

January
- Made velvet coat, padded lining for Alan.
- Learned one piece from Etude.
- Read in two Etudes.
- Outline of life of Admiral Dewey.
- Reread 8 January magazines, chiefly on resolutions.
- Did much memorizing, all I could find containing the words *strong*, *strength*, or forms thereof.

February
- Reading Lincoln in encyclopedia and old magazines.

March
- Reading William Pitt; also romance and Biography.
- Read U.S. History on French and Indian War.

April
- Read "The Turmoil," Vision of Sir Launfal.

May
- Read "The Mother of Washington," "In the days of Washington," and all about George Washington in the French and Indian War in English History. U.S. History, Chapters 4, 6, 7, 8.

July
- Learned to swim in three lessons. Swam every day rest of summer 'till cold.
- Started every other day trips to Minneapolis for medical treatment for nine weeks.
- I have strengthened my will sufficiently to overcome my fear of the water and learned to swim.

• Cause of bad complexion: neglect to <u>strengthen</u> muscles of face by daily facial massage.

October
   • Memorizing a verse of Scripture and reading its chapters every day.
   • Stevenson's "The Lamplighter" has been in my head.
   • My dressmaker said, "Anna is so little and so pretty that she can wear anything." Seems strange to me. As many times as that has been told me, I never can see it nor feel that they are quite sincere.

Other historical events of 1917:

January blizzard is worst one in 30 years (since 1887).

Temperatures dip to –20 degrees below zero.

U.S. declares war on Germany and Austria-Hungary.

1ˢᵗ Liberty Loan & War Savings certificates to meet war expenses.

Government lock & dam at Ford Bridge formally opened to navigation.

State begins to call for men to serve in WWI.

Concrete Products Company formed in Elk River by LDB and TW Longfellow.

Elk River Park Association builds a large pavilion on the fairgrounds.

January 1918

Headline: Army of U.S. Democracy a million and a half STRONG, says Baker.

Calm – peace

> *Rest*
> *The other Kewpies,*
> *Calm and mild,*
> *Each seated himself*
> *Beside a child.*

Other historical events of 1918:

The county Red Cross chapter made 566 hospital bed sheets, 599 pairs of pajamas and 2,489 pairs of socks, among other things.

The Minnesota Home Guard has 7,501 men in 58 towns by 1918.

July 1, 1918

Just been reading 10 pages of poetry (Little Book of Out-of-Doors) to my son and he went to sleep. Don't wonder at it.

April—beautiful, fresh and green, yet she weeps. Is it from pure wantonness or does she see her youth passing and foresee the work of summer, dreariness of autumn and the barrenness of winter?

Personally, I do not dread the passing of youth. The older I grow the more beauty I see in everything. At 18 years I tho't that must be the most beautiful age in a girl's life. Each following year, I tho't that must be the most beautiful. Now at 33 this month, I think the thirties are a very pleasant period, as any time before that is too immature and I have come to see many Great Truths in the last year. Looking forward, I know the coming years will be richer than any I have ever known, altho' they necessarily will hold many griefs, for, "Life is not all smiles, nor yet all tears. It admits honest laughter and needs honest tears."

I picked two crocuses from plants I bro't into my back yard the spring Alan was born. Shows what cultivation will do for wild flowers. Alice Elizabeth came to call. Talkative and cute. Her hair is exactly like Alan's. Even to the two crowns and two cowlicks in front. . .

"Fair fronds the maidenhair; in fairies realms,
The silent echo of the stately elm."

July 2, 1918

I didn't idle today, and got quite a number of things into my day—tasks and tho'ts and pleasure with my child. Accomplished one thing I had put off for weeks—giving Baby a haircut. Took me an hour while he was chasing around after a cat.

"If we knew"

If we could draw the curtain that surrounds each
  life
and see the heart and mind and purpose,
perhaps we would pity where now we blame.
Perhaps we would love the sinner tho' we loathe the
  sin.
We'd love each other better if we only understood.
That is what I have always contended and never dare
  to judge another,
because we don't know, and I can't endure to hear
  one criticized
because we might do worse if we were placed in simi
  lar circumstances.

May says, "The way of the transgressor is hard," and she has no pity, but I pity even the criminal. The more wicked, the more unfortunate the man. They have my sympathy. Never found but one person who shared my sentiment and that was Ruth Houlton (Price). She said, "Maybe we'd done the same thing in his place."

July 25, 1918

*Pepere is
Anna's Father.*

*Birthday
presents!*

I've had a visit from Jeanne and her mother and grandmother and uncle and grandfather. Pepere stayed to make me fire ladders. Had a birthday (July 14) in the meantime. I received a $15 check, War Savings Stamps, two sheets, two pillow cases, two envelope suits, a service pin and a balsam pillow.

Twenty-four hours ago, I doubted. I felt sure that I could learn to knit. But I went right at it and now I have quite an expert looking inch and three quarters. It is very fascinating, but I am afraid it is going to make my head ache.

I have been swimming quite regularly every day and I can do it quite creditably. In fact, I haven't run across anybody yet this year that can come near me. (I can brag here in private to you, Old Diary.) I went in with quite a spectacular flourish before beginners today.

August 25, 1918

One more week of summer and I have a busy week ahead finishing up scraps of sewing, a little canning, and Red Cross knitting.

Sue is leaving for Bemidji after a week's vacation and I'll have to let Alan go up to the other house, "Heartsease," to keep them from being lonesome.

"Heartsease" is the Dare ancestral home at 1237 Main Street in Elk River, where Laurence's folks lived. The author and her husband, Charles Dare, still live there today.

September 23, 1918

My reading: Ben Hur again. What a terrible thing death must be. Almost always a terrible spasm, when a soul or life leaves a body—man or animal. Especially such a violent death as the crucifixion. "My God, why hast Thou forsaken me?" Ben Hur moistened the sacred lips with wine in remembrance of the refreshing drink the Nazarene had quietly given him, when he was being led to the galleys. The face brightened, the eyes fixed with joy upon some one seen only to them in far heavens. Content, relief, even triumph. "It is finished." The head dropped and Ben Hur tho't all was over but the fainting soul recollected itself and he heard the last words spoken as to one close by, "Father, into Thy hands I commend my Spirit." A tremor shook the tortured body, a cry of fiercest anguish. The heart was broken. Of that, he died.

War Letters

1918

As the war raged in Europe, more and more of the effects of that war were being felt at home by Anna and Laurence. Laurence served in the Minnesota Home Guard, an organization started in 1917 to serve as backup to the National Guard. A letter sent to Anna added, "Your mother told us how tickled Laurence is over drilling and getting to have a uniform." Ben, Anna's brother, enlisted in the Army. Plans were that Ben's wife, Frances, and their soon to be born child, would stay with Laurence and Anna until Ben returned from military duty.

Letter from Anna's brother Ben

April 1, 1918

Dearest Sis,

We have been loafing all afternoon, raining a little every hour or so. This old camp is heavy yellow clay. Never saw so much clay in my life, real damp too. Hot during the day and colder than h— at night. I had six woolen blankets on last night. Slept in my underwear, shirt and vest, then almost froze. I never saw the beat of it.

Lars and I are pretty disappointed, Sis. We thought we had a chance to get something out of it, but we're stung. We're in with a bunch of medical men here. M.D.'s, dentists, druggists, seven or eight of them serving as buck privates, but I am stung and all I have to do is be game and stick it out.

Lars was an old schoolmate with Ben.

Maybe I'll get better later when I get out of quarantine. You know we had planned on going to Atlanta to see the bunch on Saturday and Sunday, but instead of that we came here to camp Saturday morning, expecting we could go back to town and stay until Monday, but we were shot in the arm three hours after we got here and slapped into quarantine. Don't know if we will get out of here tonight or next month. Hundreds come and go every day. I hope I go, that's all. The closer I get to the ocean the better and the sooner I go across, the better, too.

Well, Sis, tell me how the folks took it all after we left. Didn't Frances make a break for me as I was leaving, poor little sweetheart. She sure is braver than I am.

Say, Sis, when I opened that envelope, I sure did have a heart ache. Oh, well, maybe that damn Kaiser will quit soon and we can all go home. Then we can all be happy again.

Well, dear sis, don't tell Frances or ma or pa any of this, but you have always been my first aid so I had to share my troubles with you. I hope I'll hear from you soon.

Ever your Brother
Ben
Instruction Co. #2
Medical Officer Training Camp
Camp Greenleaf
Oglethorpe, Georgia

Letter from Frances, Anna's sister-in-law

April 9, 1918

Dear Anna,

We are getting lonesome for you, wish you could come and spend a day with us. We got a letter from Ben every day. I will tell you all he has told us. Perhaps you have heard from him a couple of times, though.

He just got his suitcase Thursday. While in Chattanooga, he went to the top of Lookout Mountain. It took 45 minutes to ride up to the top of it. He says he'll never forget that sight.

There is a German prison camp at Oglethorpe guarded by machine gun and barbed wire entanglement. He said they've killed eight since last fall; I imagine ones that tried to escape. We read of the authorities taking five there from New York one day last week.

Ben got his second shot in the arm Saturday. I hope it didn't make him as sick as the other one. Fort Oglethorpe is sort of a distribution center, I guess. He says he'll be moved as soon as he is through quarantine. They haven't really gotten down to their regular training yet, though they are getting some of it now.

He seems to like it. The meals are very good. Their cook has been to France and back five times since summer. He met a Frenchman from near Quebec who knows Patrick, Zita's brother, and some other cousins of yours. He is a relative of the Boutens of Minneapolis. This fellow can't talk English. I'll bet he and Ben have some good visits. Trust Ben to get acquainted.

They had quite a heavy rain there last Wednesday night, but it cooled off the weather. He says it is blistering during the day and real cool at night. He wants a sweater. So we sent to Tess to hurry up with the one she is making.

Ben is raising a moustache. He says it is quite a one as he hasn't shaved it since he left home a year and a half ago. I guess the time could go faster for him. Poor Ben, I can't bear to think of his being homesick. I'd lots rather suffer, myself.

I've been quite lonesome, but didn't cry yet. I haven't been able to go outdoors since you were here, so that makes it harder. I am going out to mail these letters this afternoon. Your mother has had quite a spell of nursing me. She surely is good to me. Couldn't be better.

We have the petticoats made and all trimmed. We got four out of the piece. The dresses are cut out. We got three out. Just finished one. I put those little medallions of yours in it. It is so sweet. I wish Ben could see them. Your mother cut them out. I'm going to scallop one at the neck and sleeves. I'll put tatting on the other.

The minister's wife had her baby Good Friday morning at the hospital. They expected her home yesterday. Don't know what sex.

Mrs. Dean gave me the prettiest pillow for a little girl, she said. It has a pretty medallion in the center and lace on the end. The pillow is pink. It shows so pretty through the white slip.

Your mother would like to go up this week, but she can't get Mrs. P. now. She got one of her spells while at Mrs. Dean's and can't work any more. So your mother is going to do a little at a time until she gets it done. She cleaned the cupboards and stove today. I wish I could help her, but I'm afraid I can't do much.

Last night is the first night I didn't cough my head off and didn't have a fever. I surely had the grippe or it had me, I don't know which.

Olive called up one day this week. She thinks you have a fine big boy. She said she and Gertie are coming over some day this week to see all the pretty things

I have for the baby. It's a good thing you gave me some things. I'll have something to show, anyway.

Joe took your mother to the Symphony Sunday. There weren't many there, I guess. It was the last one, too. He is so proud of his new car. You should have seen your mother in her grey dress. She looked so young and pretty.

Does Alan still say, "Aunty and B? I hope he doesn't forget Ben. I don't think he will, though. He'll see his picture right along. I'm anxious to get his picture in his uniform. Haven't you taken Laurence's picture in his suit yet?

Can't you drive down Sunday? We'd be so glad to see you all. Sunday was a lonesome day. I didn't think I could hold on, but I did.

Grandma sits up every day now. Isn't she doing well?

Everyone sends his love,
Frances

Letter from Ben to his wife Frances

April 20, 1918

Dearest Little Mother,

   Well, dear, I got your wire yesterday at one p.m. stating that Jeanne had arrived safely at 6:25 on the 18th. I certainly would have given my shoes to have sailed for home in an aeroplane and see my two mopps. Sure is tough not to be home when the first one comes, especially. I got a letter from Ma last night, just a few words, she wrote it Thursday morning. I wonder if my honey was very sick, and oh, dear, a lot of things I wonder at. I know that if you were sick they wouldn't tell me for fear I'd worry. Ma said it was easy for you, but I know there are no such things as easy maternity cases. I will be sick until I get a picture of you and the baby. I am most certain that you'll get excellent care as a doctor who has the heart to do the work that he did, knowing our financial condition, wouldn't neglect a thing that would help you.

   We are going to start organizing this week or next. I think the medical will be shipped to Camp Meade at Baltimore. One of the lads, the one who is on the picture with Lars and me and who works in the office, said they are going to switch the dispensary outfit and will need a druggist. He'll put my name and Lars' in. Pretty nice if he does. No drill, reveille or retreat or guard duty. I'll say it's a pipe of a job, only hope I draw it. It'll be ten days or two weeks before we do, anyway. I can stand anything now. I am through with my shots and can handle a pick and shovel, so I don't worry about anything except my family. That's the best way in the army, do what you're told, when you're told to, otherwise do as little as possible. They tell you when to eat, sleep, drink, work, and everything else. I expect a pretty good job when we get organized. I can wait 'til then.

Mother said that the baby had long black hair, so I judge she is dark. Ma said she was in love with her already, that she is pretty. The poor little honey, I'd give my shoes and walk barefoot from here to see her. I think I could get a furlough if I wanted it, but I'd have to pay my own expenses, about $50. Maybe I'll get a furlough with expenses paid later. I will if I can pull it.

You poor little Mother, having to go through such an ordeal alone. It is you who is brave. I'll tell the world that, and everyone knows it. I should be shot for leaving you when I did, but I didn't think she would come before May.

It started to rain here yesterday afternoon and we waded through yellow, red and gray clay mud until we couldn't be seen for mud. Remember the mud on that memorable ride to Chaska? That was easy to what we get here when it rains. Today is cold and dreary, and I am certainly making the best of that sweater. I have it under my shirt and it is fine, fits like a tailor-made. I got a nice box of candy from Tess, too. I wonder how they feel toward me now. I'll bet they hate the ground I ever touched. I don't blame them if they do. Maybe they'll get over it by the time I get back.

Well, honey dear, kiss our little mopp for me and take good care of yourself. Stay in the hospital until you're well enough to move. Don't hurry to save a few lousy dollars.

Ever your husband,
Ben

Letter from Frances to MeMere, her mother-in-law
(Ben & Anna's mother), while in the hospital

April 24, 1918

Dear Mother Fournier,

Ben knows Jeanne is here at last, and he is worrying how my sisters are taking it. I'm so glad May and Anne have both written since she arrived. He has their letters before now and won't need to worry about that.

This letter I just got from Ben is more encouraging than any, I think. I feel quite sure that he'll be put in the dispensary. I hope so.

I sat up to eat last night and have sat up three hours so far today. In bed, of course, but I am thankful for that. Tomorrow I can sit in the chair. Guess I can go home Saturday for sure. I'll be glad to get home, too.

Jeanne is just as good as can be. She was one of the good babies this morning, and wasn't brought until 6:00. They took those crying first. It surely is a circus to hear all the different tunes in different keys.

There are thirteen babies in the nursery now, and one is trying to be born. Isn't it the limit? I wonder where they are all coming from.

Mrs. Dean's girl was born Monday evening at six. My, but the nurse and doctor were relieved. She is feeling quite well, too. She asked one of the nurses to show her the Fournier baby. I could hear her say that Jeanne is pretty. She is almost white now.

Rose came to see her last night and Marguerite Davy came, too. They were so enthused. Didn't know that Rose would like her so much the first time. She made much more of a fuss over her than May. Rose admired every part of her, all the time she nursed.

Miss Allardyce called me up today. She is coming to see Jeanne and me Friday. Isn't everyone lovely, even though they were deceived? Ben will be so glad.

Ma didn't think Ann would be over the measles sufficient to take Jeanne Sunday, so we can have May after all. I'm so glad it has turned out that way, as you were so disappointed. May doesn't know that I asked Anne. Only Ma and Anne know that.

Uncle Will is coming again this evening and is going to bring me a box of candy, he told Ma. He is crazy to see Jeanne again, but he doesn't like the name any better. It's Ben's choice, and I wouldn't have her named anything else as long as he picked it out. I like it, too, and all the nurses think it pretty. The nurses call all the babies by their names.

How is Alan? Tell him I want him to come to see my little girl Sunday when she is dressed in her pretty clothes. I'm so anxious to have him see her. Does he remember Ben, and does he still say, "Aunty?"

How is Anna feeling, and did her cleaning turn out successfully? I hope it did. Wish she'd come Sunday.

Ma was here to mail my letter to Ben yesterday, and today before three. Saw you go by yesterday morning.

I'll be glad to have you come back. I miss your visits. But don't come before you planned to, as I'm all right and have everything I need.

Love to all,
Frances

Letter from Frances to Anna

April 27, 1918

Dear Anna,

I sat in the chair one and three-quarters hours yesterday and two hours so far today. I nursed Jeanne while sitting up today. The nurse put a pillow on my lap for her to lie on. I walked a little today, too. I'm going to get up again later this afternoon.

I can't go home before Sunday, and the doctor thought I ought to wait another week to have Jeanne baptized so perhaps you can come a week from Sunday. I'm so anxious to have Alan see the baby.

I had a letter from Ben today and he sent a picture of himself on a cannon that was used and abandoned in the Battle of Chickamonga. He still has his moustache.

They are going back to Camp Greenleaf this week, and will start their regular training as they have their officers now. He is quite confident of getting in the dispensary. I surely hope that he does. He says that as a pharmacist he won't be in danger when in France. That is, in any immediate danger.

He met a man who has been in France two years and eleven months in the Vet. Corps, and he told Ben that his work would be one of the very best jobs to be had in the whole outfit, so Ben felt pretty fine. Ben said he made some of the boys quite sick telling them of the dirty work they would have to do. He said the reason they hadn't gotten down to business before was a little spite work, but he couldn't explain further. He is very enthusiastic about his work, I think, so I feel much better. He doesn't mind the guard duty and each one has guard duty every third night as the camp is so large and there is only one company there and there is room for thirty. When they get back to Greenleaf, each one has guard duty once in three weeks. If he is in the dispensary, he won't have it at all.

It makes him lonesome to hear all about Jeanne when he can't be here, but still he wants me to tell lots about her in each letter. She is growing so much. She had her bath in the tub both yesterday and today. My nurse said all the nurses watched her because she never even whimpered, but looked around and liked it so much. I hope she'll like it when I give her the first one. I get rather nervous when I think of it.

Irene Fay came to see her last night. She thinks Jeanne the picture of Ben. Said there is no resemblance to me at all. She couldn't get over how much you could see she looks like Ben when she is just an infant.

Miss Allardyce sent me the loveliest bouquet of pink sweet peas and forget-me-nots. My, but they are lovely. She called me up again today. Isn't everyone lovely? Nell came Wednesday eve and brought me a big box of chocolates. The nurses and I had a good time eating it.

Marguerite Davy said Jeanne is Irish in her fists, at least. She handles them quite well. This morning it was so cute. She clasped her hands together and there were no two fingers of one hand together. The nurse and I laughed so. It might have been an accident that her fingers were in the right place, but she has moved those hands of hers around quite lively ever since she has been here.

I'm anxious for your mother to come back. I've missed her an awful lot. She'll probably be here to-night but I won't see her before tomorrow, I suppose.

I hope your house cleaning turned out well and that you cleaned up all the soot. Wasn't that terrible?

Ben wrote a letter to his mother, too. He gives her full charge and his share of Jeanne until he gets home. Bless his heart.

Give Alan a big squeeze for me. How is Laurence? Does he enjoy his drill work now?

Lovingly, Frances

May 2, 1918

Dearest Sis,

I received your letter last night and am much amused at the mopp performances. Does he still smoke when he hears, "B?" I wonder how he'll like the Trist cousin. I sure would give my shoes to see that little mopp of mine.

I got a telegram at guard call yesterday. I was handed one with that news, when a fellow next to me in the ranks was handed one that his mother was dead. I felt badly at not being home to be with Frances in her hour, but when I saw his telegram, I soon cheered up. It sure is rotten when it takes them 55 hours to get a telegram to a man in this damn army. A letter came almost as quickly as the wire—just four hours difference. Something rotten in Denmark, I'll say.

It certainly makes me happy to think how chummy Ma and Frances are getting. You should see the letters I get from both. I know positively that Frances loves Ma as well if not better than her own, and she tells me of all Ma does for her. That Ma is certainly an angel. All she has done for us can never be repaid in any fraction. It would certainly do Joe a world of good to get into the army for a spell. He'd do no more rocking around of chair and cursing in her presence.

I don't mind the work much now. I am all through with my shots and vaccine and feel good. We get good grub and sleep from 9 P.M. to 5:30 A.M. every night. I'm not on guard.

They had the pleasure of finding a guard with his throat cut about a week ago. They caught one of the civilians that did it. The other got away. Believe me, no one gets close enough to me nights to touch me. When they come within six paces, they're under a big .38 automatic. I take no chances. It doesn't pay.

I certainly am under your protection. Seems as though I have always been. I don't know as it's protection as much as good counsel. At any rate, I appreciate whatever you want to call it. Good counsel is often protection.

Poor Ma, she always has something to worry about. I don't think Frances takes much stock in Mrs. Davy anymore. She used to be impressed to a certain degree, but anyway, it's as well she doesn't associate with her. She is certainly some wife. I think I am certainly lucky to have such a wife, sis, mother and brother. I think my brother has improved a few thousand percent in the past couple of years. Hasn't he?

Well, Sis, they are going to start to organize this outfit in a week or so. I think Lars and I will get into the dispensary for a time. That is really a soft job. We work for about two hours in the morning, that's all.

We had a fine dinner today. Roast beef, mashed spuds, gravy, peas, celery, onions, ice cream, cookies and lemonade. Best meal I have had since I have been here. Haven't seen butter or sugar since I got here, and I am getting so I don't miss either. There isn't much variation in the chow, but it's all good when you get hungry enough. I tipped the scales at 186 last night. Not bad, is it? Here are a few snaps I took and had taken. Took some last Sunday on Lookout Mountain, 2700 feet high, but they aren't finished yet. I'll send you some when they are finished.

Well, little Sis, take good care of yourself and family, and go see the folks occasionally. I know you can always fix anything that might go wrong. Don't worry about me, as I can take care of myself fairly nice.

Ever yours, sis
Ben

November 7, 1918

Dear Sis,

Well here we are well into November and the war isn't over yet. I thought that when I saw Austria had quit that Germany wouldn't delay the game so, but they are still at it, I see. Well, personally, I hope they do fight 'til they are exhausted because that is the only way to show a Dutchman he is beat, and it sure would be a folly not to punish them now that we have them in the right place, to give it to them proper. I hope they shoot them all but one, and hang him. Sure did hand the Austrians and the Turks a lovely package and it is certain that the Germans won't get off easier, either.

Sure surprised to hear about your snowstorm. We haven't had any snow here. It rarely snows here, but is has been cold enough. We have had frosts here. They talk about cool evenings and nights, and their ocean breezes. None other than Minnesota will ever do for me, and when I get back, it's going to be worse than a world war that will jar me away from the home fires. I can't be bothered with no more wars.

I'll bet Alan can tell you where to get off at now alright. He is just about at the age where a lot of little original ideas will pop into that little blond head. Sure wish I could see you all. Wonder if he'll know me when I get back. And I am so anxious to see what my wife will do when she sees papa. Gosh, I get lonesome for her. I sure would like to see pa playing with her. Frances tells me "she likes her old Ben."

I got a letter from Joe tonight; also the one you sent me. I know exactly what barracks he is in and where he is in the barracks. He is about 200 feet from where I was in Greenleaf. He sure was lucky to have been chosen to drill the rest, 'cause he won't get any K.P. or fatigue duty. All the dirty work he'll have to do is pull up matches, cigarette butts, etc. around his quarters. I don't even have that to do here. I sure have a real job down here, and still I am far from satisfied. I want to be in France, damn it, that is what I enlisted for. Makes me laugh at Joe saying we will train for two months, then go to France. They fed us all up on all that bull for a long time till we got indigestion from it and laughed at them when they pulled it. They then quit. Those officers sure do feed us up in bull when we first came in and they fed me up well before I enlisted.

Well, Sis, the quarantine goes off in Charleston to-night at midnight and I sure hope it will lift off this camp tomorrow too. If it does, I am going to town if it is the last thing I ever do.

Well, Sis, I must quit and go get a haircut.

Love to all,
Ben

Mid-December, 1918

Dear Anna,

All the boys in the camps on this side are coming home for Christmas but ours. I don't think Ben can get here now and we were sure that Joe would be home. I will send you some of his letter.

Isn't it too bad that it turned out so bad. He was having such a good time. I didn't get a letter today and I can hardly wait for Monday to get one from him. I know he can't come for Christmas now, but I don't care if he can pull through without staying dear.

Frances went home this afternoon and couldn't come back, raining so hard, going to stay overnight. My, it's quiet when Frances and Jeanne aren't home. She got lots of things for a little tree for her. You better all come to cheer us up. It isn't too hard a trip.

I think I will get a turkey just the same because it would be lots worse. We don't think of the flu out here. Mrs. Dean took her baby to the doctor today in the streetcar. She put Vaseline in her nose. She said it was good.

Love,
Mother

Tell It to Jesus

1923-1925

The following letters written by Anna to Jesus were never meant to be viewed by other eyes. It was part of her disciplined quiet time, her time of meditation and reflection, where she could bare her soul to the God she seemed to love as much as life itself.

In these letters you'll catch a glimpse of Anna's devotion to her children. You'll remember that Daryl Dare died only a few days old in May 1909. Alan Dale Dare, mentioned in Anna's Diary, was born August 14, 1915. Two other children were also born and are mentioned briefly in this section. Charles Fournier Dare was born September 9, 1922, and Donna Mary Dare was born September 15, 1925, only seven months before Anna's death.

These letters have been included not only to share what was dear to Anna's heart, but also to lead the reader into exploring the depths of Anna's faith. Perhaps her words will give voice and encouragement to the reader's own thoughts and reflections and faith journey with God. In so doing, it is my hope that Anna may continue to do now what she so desperately longed to do during her lifetime—to help others know and experience the depth and meaning of God's great love for each of us.

If you are so moved, feel free to use the extra space in the margins in this book as a place to jot down your own thoughts and reflections as God speaks to you.

January 1, 1923

My mind is so filled with disconnected thoughts that I should write, that I cannot tell what to set down first. To begin, I must remember that I am talking to you and that no other person is hearing this any more than when I talk to you in the Blessed Sacrament. Now Charles, nearly four months old, has pulled my hair and otherwise distracted me, so I am off . . . on duty.

(Later) The thoughts I would have written then, you have received without writing and that is very well, as the purpose of my writing is to start me talking to you and keep me from pondering.

While Charles may have distracted Anna at times, it seems he also garnered his share of attention from his older brother, Alan. Here are a few of Alan's comments about his younger brother Charles:

"His initials are 'C.F.' I was thinking of naming him 'Jack' or something like that."

"Don't tell Charles he's a nuisance. Tell him he is a nice baby."

"Charles, you are cuter than we ever expected a baby to be."

January 5, 1923

The tiny, sleepy head has been kissed and put to bed. He is so sweet and smiley, and oh, how can I ever thank you for him? His lovely body and his sweet ways almost make me cry. He has fussed and rubbed and now he is quiet. You gave him to me, and many times I have offered him to you (I feel you listening now) for whatever purpose you wish to use him.

I wish both of my boys to be your servants, but I leave it to you to do with them "as thou will." You are so good to me. I cannot write the number of times that I say, "I love you, I love you."

I have long contemplated writing all my thoughts to tell you, and I thought it would make me very happy.

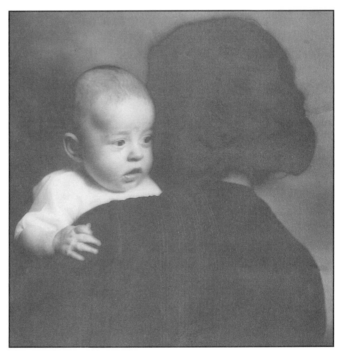

Charles Fournier Dare at three months old (1922)

January 11, 1923

Sacred Heart of Jesus, I felt this morning as though the Consecrated Host could see into the center of my being. I asked that the Precious Blood might make my soul exactly what you wanted it to be. And at the Benediction with the Blessed Sacrament, I was sure that you were blessing us exactly as you had blessed the numbers who followed you, and I felt sure, in that moment, you removed from me whatever displeased you.

Oh, Jesus. Lucy (friend) is dead. Why was it that I did not think last night to pray for those terribly hurt people? I intended to offer this morning's Mass and Holy Communion for them, but it left my mind just then, and I prayed in honor of the Holy Family, for my family. Anyway, when I heard at 11:15 that she would not live, you know I asked you that she might see her past as we all saw it, and I begged you to give her grace.

Alan, at this time seven years old, commented to his mother after communion: "I didn't really think to offer my communion for Dad but I remembered it with my inner mind, which is inside of my other mind."

January 31, 1923

My confessor says I have no serious faults, and that he has been humiliated overlooking my shortcomings too much, because he knew all my troubles. I wish he would guide me in my effort at self-improvement. Poor father, he has prayed for me untiringly and he has extricated me from all kinds of difficulties, so I will not ask him for further work for me.

It has seemed very wonderful how many times you listened to him concerning small me. When you have all of the vast universe, how can you take the trouble to even notice that I exist? Of myself, I can do nothing. I will even forget my resolutions. You can do everything for me, but I feel sure that you want me to try very hard not to depend upon you entirely to give only for the asking.

My new plan is to work by positive suggestion for one quality each month. Tomorrow, February first, I will begin to always think well, and speak well of everyone for one month. I offer my effort to you, Almighty God, and all else that I shall do this month in honor of the Blessed Trinity. Please accept my failures also, which will probably be many.

The second portion of my plan is to forget myself, and pray only for others. Not so much for individuals; but in a broader sense, if that is the way to word my ideas. The intentions of the Holy Father are about as broad as any, and I will think up some others that will especially please you, I hope.

My Jesus, I love you so much. But I must go on to my rest before one of the family wakes and expects me to do something for them. It is not self sacrifice, but duty, that makes me willing to be at their beck and call, although please remember that my duty is all joy, because it is exactly what you want me do to.

February, 1923

My God, what a struggle I have had the last few days. I'm discouraged, and disgusted with myself and in rebellion generally: a combat, indefinite in the dark . . . I don't know what. Neither will I try to analyze beyond that it began with injury at being found with many faults which I already knew, and is ending with this decision that I am sorry to have been so impatient, trusting so much to my own efforts to improve.

I will begin again by making each day tranquil and, as nearly as I am able, blameless. And I shall go to confession whenever I know that I have erred, whether it is grievous or not. Won't you please help me to remember, and teach me to succeed?

Sweet Lover of my soul, you let us have a turmoil inside, and then you give us extra quiet, besides the natural quiet that follows a storm. Nature is very clever and very kind to us in trying to repair all the damage that we foolish ones do. She follows up each outburst of emotion with the antithesis of that emotion. We call it reaction: a weeping spell is followed by uncontrollable laughter. A "let-down" feeling follows a holiday; lassitude follows excitement, etc. In each case, the reaction is to repair, to counteract in the measure in which we have spent ourselves. So unless we are on the watch, we weak ones will go from one extreme to the other.

My babe has just awakened, and I would like you to share the sweetness of him, as you loved little ones so dearly. Do you understand the joy of a mother when a tiny babe takes her face in his hands? Isn't it strange now, that he is so attracted by a face. I hold up my hand for him, and surely a hand is a wonderful thing, but he does not take it in his two hands with the affection that he takes my face. My darling boy! Five months old.

If we were holy enough to remember you every moment, we would not be swept about helplessly. So this week, in my disquiet (my physical condition may have contributed), as soon as I thought that you would rescue me in your own way, I was rewarded with more than reactionary tranquility. Jesus, you fill my soul with sweetness that I cannot define. It almost carries me, like an infant.

Please be always close to me. I need you every hour.

Oh, Master, I thought I needed you most yesterday, but I see that I need you most every day. Keep me tranquil yet a little while until a little order can come out of this Monday chaos. Here goes. . .

Ash Wednesday, 1923

It is very strange that when we begin to work on one particular thing, for character, all things seem to combine to try to make us fall down. When I first began to practice thinking well of all people, someone was determined to criticize others to me, which always lowers them in my estimation of them, even though I do not believe it. And then some force about me brought up very forcibly before me the ruination of my child by another's selfishness, but I was able to put it out of my mind. Now that I am trying to be placid, annoyances almost overwhelm me. Help me to quietly dispose of each in turn, and still the quivering of my nerves.

Easter, 1923

Dear, dear Perfect Being,

Wasn't it the cutest thing for my babe to put up his
arms for you to take him! I told him we all want to be
taken. I am very lonesome for you; how I wish I could
go alone to the church and be close to you in the Blessed
Sacrament. Please accept my illness in these strenuous days as penance in this holy season. I am sorry I
talked of quitting. How could I mention such a word,
that you are everything to me.

Furthermore, when I was separated from you before,
how I wanted you so much that I screamed aloud, coming up the stairs, "I want my God, I want my God."
Very shortly, in half an hour, you triumphed, as I knew
you would. And I promised that I would do all I could
to stay very near to you ever after. . .

Anna Delia Fournier Dare 1905

November 12, 1923

Divine Friend,

I got out of the way of writing last spring because my agony of mind was too secret to trust it on paper. Only the confessional knew. I have passed through many things in these months. Alan had flu, scarlet fever, pneumonia, paralyzed feet and paralyzed bowels. Doctors thought it would be permanent. Do you remember how I prayed at a mass at the Pro-Cathedral, Son of David, that my child may walk? And I knew in that moment that he would.

That week (March 23, 1923) we took him to Dr. Riggs, and he said, "He will get well." In the meantime Charles, at six months, had scarlet fever, bronchitis, a mastoid operation, and for three weeks we knew suspense at the possibility of double mastoid. If the pastor had not come to pray over those children, I would be childless, I know.

When I would get too bewildered to know what to do next, and what I did next might mean their lives or deaths, I had to look for guidance other than my own. O, I love you, I love you, I love you.

This digression took possession of me just as at this same time, Frances, dear sufferer, was put to bed for three months. We knew then she would never get up. I miss her terribly, but I have not been overwhelmed by her death, because, in praying for her, I never could feel that she was very far away.

I should have prayed more, only I felt sure that she was in heaven. O the pain and hopelessness and regret at leaving her four babies and a handsome husband (Ben). The last week she could not speak. Six months of continuous prayer and the remorse of conscience that I know her to have had for her sins, were what I call the privilege of purgatory on earth.

(Uncle Fred died last of August and Arthur N. Dare early in September)

November 18, 1923

Oh, you have done everything for me, and you continue from time to time to do extras. You once again relieved me from the trouble that distresses me more than all the things I dread, and made me feel composed, and after reading, "A Divine Friend," I was reminded to come to you with all my imaginings. After Holy Communion, there you were, standing before my mental vision, and I knew I had seen you look like that somewhere. It took me all day to recall that it was on my St. Rita medal. You stayed so vividly there for many days, but now I have "kind of" lost you. Won't you please come back?

Do you remember a long time ago when I was going to say some prayers after I went to bed, and I'd always fix my mind on a place across the room where you might be. This time I felt lonely at your being so far away to talk to you, and I said, "Oh, do come a little closer!" I hoped you'd come as a friend. But you certainly took me by surprise. Swiftly as thought, and seeming like the flight of a bird, you came straight into the center of my being. You did! But your visits are short, because my mind is so small that it very soon wanders to small things, and you are gone.

I really must get to sleep before Charles wakes.

November 19, 1923

Mercy, I am so irritable. And there are so many irritating things to face with two boys and a man to please. Father Seliskar says just to quit. That can be done with temper, but nerves are different. It wears me out to control them.

My Jesus dear, my king divine, you are wonderful to me! I shrank from going to receive you today because I had been impatient with each of the children, but I don't think it was anger, I did so want you that I offered the Sacrifice of the Mass by way of preparation, and then I felt sure that the general absolution would satisfy in a measure. I cannot say more, only feel.

"Eye hath not seen . . . Neither has it entered into the heart of man to understand the joys that you have prepared for those who receive you in the Blessed Sacrament! Blessed Sacrament! I thought during the mass that I could easily die (I think I would) for, or in defense of the Blessed Sacrament, if it were exposed. If I couldn't see it, I suppose that I would forget its presence as I often do in church, and get to thinking about other things. I used to find it tedious to recite the prayers to obtain a plenary indulgence for souls in purgatory, but since, I betho't me to say them in honor of the five wounds. I love, though it makes tears come, to hold each wounded hand to my lips, the feet nailed to the cross I hold tightly against my swelling bosom (nursing) and lay my head against the wounded side, and relax completely while I say my prayers at each story.

Real Presence! There is most certainly a presence. How unsatisfied we feel when we go to mass without receiving (Holy Communion). We come home feeling as though we had nothing, though we must bring home many graces and blessings from having heard mass and been in His presence. How I look forward to the elevation each time, though it scares me to think how

soon I will be at thy table and I begin to feel, "Domine,
non surr dignuus," and I think how remote I am from
being prepared. Then I know each time that, though I
should spend years in preparation, I should feel less
and less worthy, so I can only helplessly give myself
to you and let you do all.

January 2, 1924

My God, what a struggle I have been having. Why did you hide yourself so long? If you had been here, I would not have had such darkness alone, praying continually to St. Michael, to my guardian angel, to the Blessed Virgin, even to Archbishop Ireland, who always hears me. But what can they do, when your face is turned from me?

But now here you are suddenly. What peace! What sweetness! Of course, I knew that you were in the Blessed Sacrament when I received, but I could not tell you a thing that was the matter with me. Oh, sin, of course, what a price we pay for what we think are only slight offenses!

My Christmas was not a bit a happy day. I heard three masses in succession, and my mind a blank the entire time. Then I went to confession a few days later, and what a blessing that sacrament is.

Yesterday I started as a novice under the direction of your "Little Flower," St. Therese. The first chapter is on the "Love of God." Chapter 11 is all about "Love of Neighbor." Then I decided to recite an act of love every few minutes, and I thought you would like me to read the Psalms for praise. You told me once, "That is just what I want you to do."

So you came quite suddenly, to console me. You are so good to me, and you give me such sweet and frequent consolation that sometimes, I fear that I will not have much reserved for me in heaven. I am getting it all here!

But just at this time, Jesus, I need you particularly. Stay with me by the grace. Let me see you night and day for some time. "Do keep us near to thee, and make our hearts so like to thine that we may holy be."

January 13, 1924

I do not know by what name to call you this time, to
express my dependence: supreme guide and compan-
ion? You have not been so inaccessible of late, and I
am glad that I learned one thing today from Petite
Therese, that you can always be reached through your
sacred heart. I must learn her very words concerning
it.

How happily I was godmother to my communicant
last week, and what a perfect confession she made. I
never saw a penitent like that. She came out, appar-
ently unseeing and walking automatically. She came
to my arms and would have been satisfied to stay there.
. . I leave her now to you. Can you find it in your heart
to be her strength? She wants to be good, but she needs
strong authority and constant watchfulness.

In the meantime, I had an excuse to relax my vigil
once on my worst failing, so I had to begin my struggle
over again these days. But I feel sure you will come to
my aid if I request your presence every few minutes.

February 21, 1924

Jesus, I place within your sacred heart all my thoughts and actions, especially those which displease thee. As a careful mother seizes a dangerous tool from her child and hides it in her bosom, so you, also, please snatch from me all that is harmful to me and hide it to be consumed by love.

February 22, 1924

My love, You are so wonderful to me to give me a little understanding of the cause of my spiritual struggles. For some time I was oppressed with thoughts that shamed me, and would have made me distracted if they had lasted longer than minutes. Now they have left, and I was made to think I had made a bad confession. I felt as though you frowned upon me, though you gave me moments of sweetness. Also, I thought I should not communicate, but my loneliness overcame my fear, and there you made me see that the adversary was pestering me with that anxiety to keep me from the Sweet Sacrament, or at least to make me less fervent. I am glad that I am free again.

O Jesus, come and take such complete possession of me that there will be no room left for anything that displeases you. I belong to you entirely, so much so that if you wished to take me in one of the blissful times, I should fly to you and forget children, husband and all, and I would not think of my Judge, but my thought is that I should be steeped in the love of God for all eternity. My soul nearly bursts with love.

That is the way (easiest) that I choose to die, because what I fear most is that you may hide yourself from me in my last moments, and then I would fear much, and my faith might vanish. I can only hope that you will do what is best for me, so that I may not perish. Remember that it was all very well for you to try your Saints, because you knew that would endure and triumph. But you also know me, that I must be supported always, or I'll fall off by the wayside.

April 23, 1924

How I love the Blessed Sacrament. I think of the little white host, and my soul beams rapturously! Certainly there is a power about it past understanding. Though I begin to see a little of the "Little Flower's" meaning of love, always love, it is still a little too vague for me to put it down.

"God is love." So in frequent Holy Communion, we receive so much love and it keeps accumulating so that we grow to love not only God, but we love our fellows more. That is the explanation for the affection for my spiritual daughter, and how much more I love my husband. And were I used to get secretly into a fury over small criticisms, I was able not long ago to cry without bitterness over injustice from May, and later tell her she is good to me.

Just yesterday I was able to grasp a little of Mary's love for us, and I was happy in my resulting love for her. In the way that I have just understood that we receive love for our fellows by being allowed a few blissful moments with our Savior, she, by her sufferings for us and her submitting her body that He might be, along with her solicitous care of Him all the years of His life, her soul was enlarged sufficiently to embrace all of her spiritual children, and little we appreciate her love. How little, too, we appreciate her sacrifice. A sacrifice is joy if it is appreciated, but the bitterest bitterness if it is overlooked.

As I have found out, the people for whom we make the largest sacrifices are the ones who like us the least. I imagine Mary's love for Jesus, and imagine her seeing his mutilated body. When we love a person, we love their personalities, but we never think of their bodies.

But a mother loves her child's body, every line and inch of it, and to see it thinning, or ever so slight an imperfection of a member makes her sore to the core.

It starts a fever of dread. I know Mary's dread and rapid breath at Simeon's prophecy, and I know that it clung heavily on, while she continued about her duties. Then, imagine traveling to Egypt with a huge babe, not in a closed car, and with insufficient clothing, and the horror hanging over their heads that at any moment they might be discovered, and with that prophecy still fresh in their minds. I say "They," now, because poor St. Joseph doesn't get enough credit for his share in the care and anxiety for the Christ Child. . .

April 29, 1924

"I can do all things in Him who strengthened me."
That is true. How long have I been trying to get Lad to
do a matter that I could not bring myself to do, and
finally, I said, "Well, I will have to have help from the
Holy Ghost; I leave it to Him." When I had finished
my rosary on my way home, it came about easily and
naturally, to tell him all.

I can't see how I happened to forget that it was the
Blessed Virgin who brought my husband to Baptism....
Do you remember the decades and decades of Hail
Mary's I recited the winter before my marriage, and
the Mother, in a blue mantle, was always before my
mental vision everywhere I went, especially on my long
rides with my white horse?

May 25, 1924

My Jesus, it seems to me that I love you more every day. O, why are you so wonderful to me? I thank you for giving me a growing affection and confidence in your sweet mother. I have a new plan now. Let me know it, because it feels like a rare success. I have consecrated myself to her, so that she will prepare my soul for you.

Who can know better than she what you want me to be. So, from now on I will be in her hands, being guided and molded into the being that you expect me to be. She prepared me for Holy Communion this morning, and she did it so well, without any violation of mine, that I am always going to let her do it henceforth.

She was my matron of honor at first, robbing me properly to go to meet the bridegroom. But there I felt so helpless and so little, that I decided to be a very small, scared girl like on my first communion, and my beautiful, loving, solicitous mother carefully, protecting, led me to the Great Master, and He stooped down to me. Oh, why are you so wonderful to me? It makes me cry.

That part of my plan is not the most consoling. Though I love God so much, I am always afraid to die, because there will be so many reproachful things on the bad side of the ledger. But now I think that if the Blessed Virgin always leads me to her divine Son in the Blessed Sacrament, I will ask her lovingly, protectingly, to lead me to Him when I die, and she will not let me be judged harshly.

I have also chosen St. Anne, her mother the blessed Theresa, who is very dear to me, and my patroness, St. Rita. These three will be her attendants wherever she leads me. I will be glad to see them, and when God sees them looking out for me, and all our love for each other and Him, He will let me stay in heaven.

July 23, 1924

Dear Jesus, my love. I so long for all good and I so despise all my faults and weaknesses that they make me feel ill. Certainly they make me sick at heart. And I wish that you would come and take so complete possession of me that I would never be conscious of evil anywhere in the world.

If I were to surrender myself to the enemy in the yearning way that I throw myself at you, he would not be slow in claiming me, and I should know nothing of God, but only wretchedness. In the same way, then, why does not the son of God want me when I want Him so much? Because of my imperfections, of course. But you can transform me easily by your own perfections, and then I should be all-pleasing to you. You know that I cannot gain an inch by myself, so I leave it to you to do all for me in your own way and in your own time. It must be your way to let me struggle with the things I despise, though it seems to me degrading, rather than that I am gaining strength.

I wish there could be nothing to distract me but just contemplating your sweetness. Even though I like to sleep (night is the only time I have to pray), I could give up much of it if weariness did not make me lose control the next day. (I think "perpetual adoration" would satisfy me better than anything I think of, but I can't expect to have brought to me here.) Please keep my desires always in mind, and I will try to be patient. I love you.

Sweet Love, I feel happier today than I have for I don't know how long. I don't dare to think of it for fear it will change. It seems to me nothing would matter if I could arrange to go to the cross and receive Holy Communion. Every day, for some years, matters have gradually arranged themselves so that I could go more and more often, and now I see a possibility that I may be able to go every day, at least during the milder months. I thank you with my soul for each thing that has contributed to my freedom. I think that was the last obstacle.

December 17, 1924

Precious Friend, it has been several months since I
could write to you. The last time I wrote was the happiest day, spiritually, that I have known, and like words,
work's joy being marred by anticipating that sorrow
would follow, so I felt that such bliss was perhaps "not
so good." I was mistaken, as you know. A little ner-
vousness and a few hasty words precipitated a deluge!
I won! I have been to Mass and sweet communion almost every day since, but I have not always felt satisfied, and I have wondered that I was sometimes so
cold and erring. How I despise my irregularities . . .

January 1, 1925

Jesus, I wish that my talks with you were not so suddenly interrupted. Yet, it's all very well because you know all that I was going to tell you, and it is just for my enjoyment of you that I want to put it down here. But it would be convenient to sometimes refer to my past thoughts, for I seldom have them more than once.

I am grateful to you for innumerable things in the Old Year. I see clearly, as the Pastor says, that you are not going to be outdone in generosity. Every such thing that I tried to do for you, you rewarded so many fold that I never knew that it could be . . .

May 1925

Four months of nausea, sickeningly, and distressing finances. I knew long, continued gnawing pain until I thought that even the opening of heaven before me could not give me pleasure. How languidly and dumbly I sat gazing at the Blessed Sacrament during Lenten devotions.

Consolations. It was my own choice that I have this coming babe. I have given to God my body, including my sore, sore breasts that he needs also later, to use in his work of creation.

June 20, 1925

I had the chance to make my four visits a day on twenty constructive days. Holy Year Indulgences. Some days the stairs were endless; my avoirdupois and my terribly paining heart! Some days it seemed impossible to make arrangements to go to church at all, but always it was permitted.

Blessed Sacrament, because I love you, it makes me suffer to think of the years I might have enjoyed you frequently, and it makes me nearly scream to think of all the souls who might be ecstatically having you now. How much they are missing, and how much of adoration you are losing. At least, I thank you for the souls who were receiving you this morning, who were so involved that they all seemed to forget to leave the Table of the Lord. When I looked up, the pastor was continuing with the Mass, way past communion.

September 1, 1925

My Beloved! This is just the time when my patroness, St. Anne, was awaiting the coming of her holy
daughter with the same anxiety and discomfort that I
am experiencing. I regard it a wonderful privilege to
be permitted to unite my sufferings with hers, and offer them to you. Sanctify thee, and keep them for your
own purposes.

I have decided to make of these last days a novena,
in honor of St. Anne and the daughter of Anne, as nearly
perfect as I can. Beginning with my Holy Communion this morning, I see solitude, silence, prayer, calm,
and doing for others. As the story of her life tells that
she chose several holy women to assist her, I have asked
her and her daughter, St. Rita, and the Little Flower, to
be my companions during these waiting days you have
let me have them, especially Good St. Anne, whom I
feel to be particularly sympathetic and loving.

September 2, 1925

How shall I ever do without you in the coming year, when I cannot leave a little nursing babe to go to mass every day? I have planned that, if possible, by way of recreation, I shall have the car for an hour out of the 24 that I am "on the job," and take the children to the church for a visit and prayers. I may not be able to arrange it, but usually when I want something for you, you arrange it in time. Oh, it has been such a scorching day that I am quite wilted. But now the wind has turned, so we can breathe and can get clothed before my lover comes home from his strenuous day.

Poor "dear Dad," take care of him and give him time to know you better. Surely, a man who all his life has done exactly what he thought was right, you will not let him do without you. As his schoolmate, as his sweetheart, and as his wife, I have never known him to do a thing that, according to his standards would displease you, because you see him. So I offer to you his integrity, his rigid conscience, his love for me, and his work, and his tremendous sacrifices for his parents, that you may give him a wonderful love for you.

September 3, 1925

This hot day seemed unbearable until I thought that it could be much worse in many ways. You made me see a thing today at mass that I thank you for. I have long regretted that I did not join some sisterhood. I would have been spared so many hardships, my girl-hood faults would have been corrected, as I could have gone to you with an innocent heart and an open, loving face.

There is not a doubt but that I had a vocation, as my pastor knew, but he never spoke of it to me. I did not have the stamina to mention my longing. Even two years ago, the Mother of a convent insisted that I had many of the make of a vocation and scorned my choosing the world. I did not choose, I drifted.

Fortunately, I was given the purest man on earth. While I was pondering these regrets at mass today, you made me see that you wished me to drift and err thereafter, suffer mentally from many things as no one I know has endured in absolute secret. So now I come to you each day as I will on my last day in fear, and shame-faced like Mary Magdalene. That you loved her is my only hope. Help me!

Every day I grow much more helpless. The pains in my flesh grow more frequent and more sharp. Pressure on my nerves from weight and motion, floor me literally many times a day. Every step is fearfully painful, and many times I go upstairs like a dog. Going to another room seems like a journey. I would not feel that I could bear it, if I didn't bear in mind that it is all for you. The words of "Nearer My God to Thee," have never meant so much to me, as I think every step and every pain brings me nearer to you, if you give me the grace to "persevere to the end." I am sorry that I felt some rancor over a remark that was trivial. Sweet love, you are so good to me.

September 5, 1925

I felt abused at being left alone again all day, and still felt selfish about spoiling their holiday.

I feel encouraged when at last the pastor understands one thing I have been trying to make him help me with for years. . .

September 6, 1925

Through a very uncomfortable night, you came three times to console me, and I was able to once more go to Sunday mass. Much as I dreaded to appear conspicuous, I was able to forget myself and, if it is indelicate, at least our books tell us to dress as nicely as we can when we go out among our friends for the good of our spirits.

I certainly was proud of Big Son, Alan. . . He looks like an angel at his weekly communion. He just beams, and clings to me as you bring our souls nearer to your heart. Ten years old and innocent as a babe in his secret with mother that we would "get ready in case" you sent us a new baby.

"My, won't Dad be surprised?"

September 7, 1925

Dear Jesus, I think of your wounded heart these months when my poor womb, all dilated under double duty, tries to tear itself open until I strap it to take the knives out of it.

In the three and a half years that I have made the way of the cross daily, I have gradually become much attached to and more dependent on some certain stations, but always wished I could omit the Fifth, because it seemed entirely unimportant to me. The last year was very forcibly brought me to understand what its lesson to us can be, and I would have been overwhelmed many times more than I was, if you had not kept remembering the Fifth Station. Oh, Miserere!

September 8, 1925

Nativity of the Blessed Virgin Mary. Three years ago today, how hard I worked that Charles might be born on that day, because I was so sure he was a girl I wanted to name Mary. I walked up and down the yard all night in labor and half the next day, but you knew better, and I was glad to put it off a day when he turned out to be masculine.

This time, though, I hope to have a baby daughter born on that day. I know better than to be so eager about it, because if it is a boy, I prefer to have it on Charles's birthday, September 9, if it pleases you. I am entirely unworthy of so tremendous a favor as to be an Anne, born on a Tuesday in July and have a Donna Mary, born on September 8. So, I have learned this much resignation. I thank you.

September 9, 1925

I remember three years ago when Charles was coming. It was just past midnight with pains coming fast. Charles was such a joy today with his birthday presents!

September 10, 1925

By radio: "To keep yourself sweet and be superior to the annoyances of the day."

Susan told me my lavender dress is too long. Even small criticisms like that disturb me. I said not a word, because I wanted to tell you, diary, my defense. That for the purpose I want it, it is just right. My shorter dresses make me look too big around. If there is anything I despise to see, it's a woman in the last weeks wearing skirts below the knee. May did say that she "never saw anyone go though a period like that and keep looking pretty to the last."

I disregard fashions and dress according to my needs...long straight lines to give length and large enough sized garments to hang down straight without revealing a bulge.

My spiritual advisor told me to say one Our Father and Hail Mary when anything rankled inside. I don't always remember to do that, but if I write it here, it is an outlet and no one need know but you.

September 15, 1925

At 11:15 on September 14, 1925, when I had the first unmistakable contraction, I had as much courage as an infant, until I thought of the date—that my anguish would be on September 15. So, uniting them to the seven sorrows of your patient mother, I offered all to you. And my dread left me completely.

And I called the nurse and doctor, heated water for sterilizing, warmed the bathroom for the babe, and at 2:15 A.M. Donna Mary was in the world . . .

November 1, 1925

All Saints Day. I will lift my soul so high! That I cannot feel the scorn and plight that some hand out to me.

"Dear God, thank you for Li'le Gi'l." – Charles

Sunday November 29, 1925

"How swift I turned attentive,
My soul aflame with prayer!"

I longed to be Thine alone! I longed to be perfectly
united to Thee! I longed so intensely that I supported
exceedingly and immediately when you answered me
by reminding me of my custom of frequent spiritual
Communions. The words that have satisfied me:

"Jesus Christ, come into my soul. Take complete
possession of my being, so that all my thoughts and
words and actions—my sleep, my heartbeats and my
breathing, even, may be exactly in accordance with
Thy holy Will."

Further, you made me see that my body would stay
here to sash and dress children, order a household and
all that I am needed for, while I could be with you. I
wish that I were strong minded enough to hold that
thought twenty-four hours a day. I would like to go to
mass and be conscious of nothing except the Presence
in the tabernacle. How feeble we are to know beyond
the shadow of a doubt of this Presence, and still we
wander.

How good you are! How well you understand us and
carry us along like infants that we are, not even conscious that we need you!

Sacred Heart, how wonderful you are in straighten-
ing out affairs. I will give up my sleep today while the
children sleep to tell you about how you gave me back
my best friend. . .

A note from Laurence

February 5, 1926

Anna doesn't feel well today. Her head is throbbing. The weather matches the solemn mood of this household; it is dreary, cold, and snowing. We visited the doctor yesterday and he doesn't know what is wrong. He thinks it's an ear infection. But do ear infections make someone bedridden? I am overcome with concern for her that it is more than an infection. But how do you challenge a doctor's diagnosis? I don't know what to do. Anna seems to get worse as the days go by. It's hard to see her in so much pain. And the little ones, they cry often for their mamma to be happy. Please God, make her well again!

Notice in the Star News

Mrs. L.A. Dare was taken to Hillcrest Hospital in Minneapolis on Wednesday of last week, suffering with ear trouble, and an operation for mastoiditis was performed. She is slowly recovering her strength. This is the second time she has gone through this painful experience.

Hospital stays were not always pleasant experiences. Anna's mother-in-law, May, wrote this account while in the hospital in Minneapolis, Minnesota, in the 1890s:

Three o'clock sounds solemnly from the clock in the tall church tower opposite, and morning is yet far off. Here and there through the hospital wards a weary sufferer turns upon a sleepless pillow, and sighs for the dawn; the dawn that, alas, for some of them, may never break.

Softly the night nurse moves to and fro, smoothing the pillow for one; holding cooling draught to the parched lips of another and doing all with that quiet, unselfish patience only found among the sisters of charity. These are the noble women who have renounced all selfishness and devoted their lives to ministering to the suffering.

Four o'clock sounds, and the weary watcher knows that her vigil is about ended, for at five another sister will take her place. As the hour draws near, she goes from couch to couch filling the glass upon each little stand drawn up by the narrow cot, with water fresh and pure. Eagerly the thin hands grasp it, and never nectar tasted sweeter than this cold water to those parched lips.

Away from there, crowded wards in one of the private rooms of the hospital, lies an invalid who has been watching the grey, ghostly light steal in at the closed shutters, lighting the bare painted walls as it brightens. As she watches, she thinks how this same grey light is stealing in her cozy chamber at home, and longs to be there.

The door opens, and a white-capped sister enters, softly, lest she find her patient sleeping. In hushed tones she tells of one poor woman who has just died in one of the wards leaving at home a family of nine motherless children, the youngest but two years old. And the repiner upon the bed, while saddened at the tale, yet thanks God in her heart at the contrast in her own lot, so soon to return to happy home and friends.

Five, six and seven o'clock are tolled forth, and the active bustle of the day has commenced in the halls and corridors of the hospital. The cook and the janitor go to their work, the different nurses to their breakfast, and our repining invalid soon learns to tell the step of each. At eight, the breakfast trays for the patients are carried around. Nourishing, yet plain food, and the repiner brightens visibly under its influence, and begins to think the battle of life not quite so hard, after all.

At nine the firm, resounding steps of the doctors are heard in the halls. Here and there they go, cheering and relieving their patients with hearty, kind words for each one. One portly gentleman in particular, is followed everywhere by an equally portly spaniel dog, which must enter every room, seemingly quite as interested in each patient as his master.

At ten the doctors depart, to reappear at noon, when normally one or more poor sufferers are conveyed to that upper room, that chamber of horrors, the operating room, there to be prepared to become better or—worse, as a Higher Power alone wills.

As the afternoon wears on, visitors drop in to relieve the tedium of the weary hours, some bringing flowers, perhaps, or books and papers for those who are able to read. A poor little girl in one of the wards who has no one to visit her, turns wearily to the nurse and whispers, "Will you write for me today?"

"Write for you, dear? Indeed yes. What shall I write?"

"Ask them to send me another little card." And the large eyes fill, with the very effort to be patient over the simple, ungratified wish.

Thus, amid screams at times sad and heartrending, at intervals cheerful and bright, as in life everywhere, the day draws to a close. The gas is lighted, the invalids are made as comfortable as possible for the night, and the clock in the tower tolls on with solemn note, and another weary day is done. But if borne with patience, who shall say that such a day is wasted from our life?

Anna's Obituary in the Star News

April 15, 1926

Mrs. L.A. Dare passed away last Friday morning at Hillcrest Hospital in Minneapolis, death coming as a relief to the great suffering through which she had gone during the past month. She made a brave fight for life, though she realized more than anyone else that her recovery was doubtful.

Four weeks ago Mrs. Dare was taken to the hospital suffering with mastoid trouble. An operation was immediately performed and she appeared to be making progress toward ultimate recovery. A little over two weeks following the operation, she suddenly became worse and from that time suffered terribly, a brain abscess, it is believed, causing her death Friday morning.

Mrs. Dare, who before her marriage was Anna Fournier, was born on a farm near Dayton and was 40 years of age. She spent her early childhood at Dayton, later moving with her parents to a farm in Otsego, where she lived until her marriage. She attended the Elk River high school, graduated in 1905 and married in 1907, living for brief periods at Duluth, North Branch, and Minneapolis, before returning to Elk River in 1911.

Besides her husband, Mrs. Dare is survived by three children, Alan, age 10, Charles, age 3, and Donna Mary, age 7 months; her parents, Mr. and Mrs. Hubert Fournier, of Minneapolis, and two brothers, Dr. J.C. Fournier, of New York, and B.E. Fournier, of Elk River.

A favorite poem of Anna's
(Author unknown)

Just being happy is a fine thing to do;
Looking on the bright side rather than the blue;
Sad or sunny musing is largely in the choosing,
And just being happy is brave work and true.

Afterwords

Laurence continued working at the Star News as owner/publisher after Anna's death. The following is an article Laurence wrote on June 15, 1933, titled "Memories of Other Days in Elk River."

The Houlton Sawmill

While Elk River was just outside the big pine woods district of Minnesota, the timber line being about twenty-five miles north, it was from the early days known as a sawmill town and millions of feet of high grade lumber were manufactured here.

There was a sawmill located on the bank of the Mississippi river about where the bridge now spans the river at least sixty years ago, but this mill operated only a few years and it was the lumbering business at upper town that was the most successful and of which I retain a very vivid memory.

The Houlton sawmill was located about three quarters of a mile southwest of the bridge across the Elk river at upper town, on what was known as the sawmill slough, a branch of the Mississippi circling a large island. In this slough the logs from up river designated for the Houlton mill were diverted and stored for the mill. A small dam was built below the mill to hold up the water level to float the logs in the slough.

The mill was a large two-story structure containing all the machinery necessary for the manufacture of lumber of all kinds, including lath and shingles. It was a place of great interest to the boys of that day and the irregular drone of the big saws and the screech of the smaller ones, the rumble of the conveyors back and forth, the swish of the steam from the huge boilers and whirr of the pulleys and belting produced a conglomeration of noise which will probably never be forgotten by the youths who frequently visited the big mill.

Logs Easily Handled

Of chief interest was the log elevator which conveyed the logs from the river up into the mill and piled them beside the huge saw. We were always interested in the method of handling the giant logs and the ease with which the rivermen could place them where they wanted them and the mechanical "nigger" which tossed the logs into position on the saw carriage with ease when operated by the expert carriage men. And it was something of a thrill when the big saw bit into the log at a furious speed, sometimes being slowed up temporarily when a knot came in contact with it.

As the log was sawed up the lumber was thrown upon conveyors which ran the length of the building and expert mill men would separate the best and shove the boards on to other conveyors to be properly trimmed, while the poorer pieces would continue on to be sawed up for pine wood kindling, and some of the slabs were made into shingles.

At the end of the mill huge dump carts were stationed and the waste slabs were piled directly into these and taken to the dumping yards or delivered directly to customers about town at the small sum of 75 cents a load. Incidentally, the boys and girls of that day nearly always had a pile of pine wood in their back yards to pile up and it was rather ornery job as one's hands became full of splinters.

A City of Lumber

North of the mill on the level ground, now a part of the Houlton farm, was a veritable city of lumber piles with long narrow streets and what seemed to us in those days to be regular skyscrapers of lumber on each side. It was great fun to climb these piles of lumber and walk from

Laurence A. Dare, editor, Sherburne County Star News (about 1930)

one to another. The lumber yard extended for half a mile and millions of feet of lumber were piled there awaiting seasoning before shipment.

At the northwest side of the yard were the piles of slabwood ready for delivery to people in town. When the mill closed and the lumber yard was finally abandoned there was still a large pile of kindling wood there and for many years local people could go there and dig up slabs. Probably there is some of it there yet.

On a hillside facing the city-like stretch of lumber yard was an old shack or shanty occupied for many years by a man named Farris Cooley, quite a character, who sometimes succumbed to the influence of John Barleycorn, and was greatly feared by the children, although a good fellow at heart. He was something of a veterinarian and made his living by doctoring horses.

Lumber Finished at Planing Mill

At the north end of the lumber yard was situated the planing mill, also a part of the Houlton lumbering business, where the finishing touches were put upon the rough lumber. This too was another interesting place. This mill was originally operated by water power, but later more power was needed and a steam plant was built as an auxiliary unit.

Altogether, with the sawmill going at full tilt, oftentimes all summer long night and day, the planing mill and the huge flour mill, upper town at Elk River was a very busy manufacturing center and many families earned their livelihood in one or the other of the industries.

One can still find a few ruins of the old sawmill, the brickwork of the boiler room, a few pulleys strewn about , but there isn't a vestige left of the lumber yard, now all a part of the Houlton farm, and little is left to show the site of the planing mill. The sawmill was torn down over a quarter century ago and the planning mill burned down about a dozen years ago.

But as one of the boys of that era in Elk River's history, I retain a very vivid picture of the whole busy scene and would like once again to hear the deep toned sawmill whistle and the drone of the saws and would like to pass through the fresh-scented lumber yard, and even have a pile of fresh pine wood in the back yard to split and pile. But the day of the lumbering business in Elk River passed many years ago and memory will have to serve to bring back the days of Elk River's greatest manufacturing activity.

Epilogue

Laurence sat in the back seat with me as we motored from Minneapolis to Elk River on a rainy fall evening in 1972. I had known him only in his later years, a gentle, peaceful man full of deep silent memories.

This was my father-in-law. At 87, he still lived at Riverview, the cottage he shared since 1912, first with Anna, and after her death, with his second wife, Rose.

Now Rose sat in the front seat talking to Charlie. The radio lent a brass accompaniment and covered our lowered voices. We shared a lap blanket.

I ventured a family question: "I have wondered what Anna was like."

A tender smile in response was suddenly erased by pain of recollection. His mouth was set.

"It was a long time ago."

"How did you meet her," I asked a few miles later, "and when?"

"I don't remember." It was too quick.

There was a lengthy pause as I sensed the fragility of long-repressed memories of people, times and places. I looked down and pondered the new life within me. Then I asked what he thought about his son becoming a father at fifty. He smiled and told me that his last child was born when HE was fifty.

After a bit, I thought of my child's grandmother of whom we all knew so little.

"Was she pretty?" I quietly asked.

Again to his lips stole that gentle smile, as he nodded yes. At the same moment, big tears filled his eyes and coursed slowly down the dear old cheek. With a determined effort he spoke.

"Yes. Yes, she was."

Under the blanket I touched his arm, and we held hands in the tranquil darkness all the way home.

Sally Anne Dare

Bibliography

D'Entremont, Rev. Clarence J. "New Findings on the Melansons," French Canadian and Acadian Genealogical Review, Vol. II, No. 4 (Winter 1969).

_____. "The Melansons of Acadia Had a French Father and an English Mother," French Canadian and Acadian Genealogical Review. Vol. VI, No. 1 (Spring 1978).

Folwell, William Watts, A History of Minnesota, Volumes I and II. St. Paul: Minnesota Historical Society, 1956.

Goodrich, Albert M. History of Anoka County and the Towns of Champlin and Dayton in Hennepin County, Minnesota. Minneapolis: Hennepin Publishing Co., 1905, pp. 175-176.

Herbin, John Frederic, The History of Grand-Pre: The Home of Longfellow's "Evangeline." (4th ed.) Bowie: Heritage Books, Inc., 1991.

History of Hennepin County: Dayton. pp. 1352-1360.

History of Wright County, Two volumes.

Inskip, Leonard. "Minnesotans Learn About State's Rich, But Quiet, French Heritage." Minneapolis Star and Tribune, November 17, 1985.

Sherburne County Star News. Miscellaneous issues, 1900-1907.

Plat maps of Dayton, Minnesota. Minneapolis: Hennepin History Museum.

Obituary of Magloire DeMars. Osseo Press, May 27, 1924.

Sorensen, Tom, "The Old Farm Dates Back To Great-great-grandpa." Minneapolis Star and Tribune, September 13, 1980, p. 1B.

Thacker, Robert. "Pembina Pioneers."

"Town of Dayton Early Trading Post." Minneapolis Journal, November 24, 1938.

Upham, Warren, "Minnesota Geographic Names: Dayton." Minnesota Historical Society, Volume XVII. St. Paul: Minnesota Historical Society, 1920.

Yzermans, Vincent. Between Two Rivers: A Centennial Narrative of St. Andrew's Parish. Waite Park: Park Press, 1991.

Order Form

Please fill out this form (or copy this page), add the necessary information, and mail it to:

> DeForest Press
> P.O. Box 154
> Elk River, MN 55330

Please enclose personal check or money order, payable to: DeForest Press.

Anna: Letters from the Attic $14.95 each

Qty. _____   Total: _____

Minnesota residents add 6.5% sales tax   _____

Shipping & Handling: Add $2.00 per book   _____

Total enclosed   _____

Name: _____

Address: _____

City: _____ State: _____ Zip: _____

Phone: (_____) _____

Email: _____

____ Yes, please send me information about your other books, greeting cards, and posters.

You can also order this book and others from our secure web site at:
www.DeForestPress.com for immediate delivery